ADVERSITY & GRACE

ADVERSITY & GRACE
Marianne Moore
1936–1941

EDITED BY HEATHER CASS WHITE

Introduction and notes copyright
© 2012, Heather Cass White.

ELS Editions
Department of English
University of Victoria
Victoria, BC, Canada
v8w 3w1
www.elseditions.com

Founding Editor: Samuel L. Macey
General Editor: Luke Carson

Book design by Jason Dewinetz.

Printed by CreateSpace.

No part of this publication may be reproduced, stored in a retrieval system or transmitted, in any form or by any means, without the prior written consent of the publisher or a licence from The Canadian Copyright Licensing Agency (Access Copyright). For an Access Copyright licence, visit *www.accesscopyright.ca* or call toll free to 1-800-893-5777.

LIBRARY AND ARCHIVES CANADA
CATALOGUING IN PUBLICATION

Moore, Marianne, 1887–1972
    Adversity and grace : Marianne Moore, 1936–1941 / edited and with an introduction by Heather Cass White.

(ELS monograph series, ISSN 0829-7681 ; 107)
Includes index.
ISBN 978-1-55058-390-8

  1. Moore, Marianne, 1887–1972--Criticism and interpretation.
  I. White, Heather Cass
  II. Title.
  III. Series: ELS monograph series ; 107

PS3525.O5616A73 2012
811'.52   C2012-900431-6

For copyright reasons, this edition is only for sale in the United States, its territories and dependencies, the Philippines and Canada.

Lines from "What are Years," "Light is Speech," "He 'Digesteth Harde Yron,'" "Walking-Sticks and Paperweights and Watermarks," "The Student," "Half-Deity," "Smooth Gnarled Crape Myrtle," "Bird-Witted," "Virginia Britannia," "See in the Midst of Fair Leaves," "Spenser's Ireland," "Four Quartz Crystal Clocks," "The Pangolin," "The Paper Nautilus," and "Rigorists" reprinted with the permission of Scribner, a division of Simon & Schuster, Inc., from *The Collected Poems of Marianne Moore* by Marianne Moore. Copyright © 1941 by Marianne Moore; copyright renewed © 1969 by Marianne Moore. All rights reserved.

Selections from unpublished letters and artwork of Marianne Moore are used by permission of David Moore, Esq., Executor of the Estate of Marianne Moore.

For my parents, who taught me how to read.

TABLE OF CONTENTS

ACKNOWLEDGMENTS — *ix*
INTRODUCTION — *xi*

WHAT ARE YEARS — *1*

FIRST PRESENTATIONS
    Abbreviations — *74*
    A Note on the Apparatus — *75*

"The Student" — *77*
    variant table — *83*
    facing-page comparison 1932–1941 — *84*

"Half Deity" — *88*
    variant table — *91*
    facing-page comparison 1936–1941 — *92*

"Smooth Gnarled Crepe Myrtle!" — *98*
    variant table — *99*

"Virginia Britannia" — *101*
    variant table — *107*

"The Pangolin" — *113*
    variant table — *118*

"See in the Midst of Fair Leaves" — *119*
    variant table — *120*

"Bird-Witted" — *121*
    variant table — *122*

"Walking-Sticks and Paperweights and Watermarks" — *123*
    variant table — *129*
    facing-page comparison 1936–1941 — *130*

"Four Quartz Crystal Clocks" — *141*
    variant table — *143*

"A Glass-Ribbed Nest" — *145*
    variant table — *147*

"What Are Years?" — *148*
    variant table — *149*

"Rigorists" — *150*
    variant table — *152*

"Light is Speech" — *153*
    variant table — *154*

"Spenser's Ireland" — *155*
    variant table — *157*

"He 'Digesteth Harde Yron'" — *158*
    variant table — *161*

ANNOTATED LIST OF ILLUSTRATIONS — *163*

WORKS CITED — *167*

INDEX OF POEMS — *169*

ACKNOWLEDGMENTS

I thank the W.S. Hoole Special Collections Library at the University of Alabama for purchasing and allowing me to reproduce poems from an original copy of *The Pangolin and Other Verse*. Chris Petter, at the University of Victoria, made the scanning of all the other poems possible. Jason Dewinetz worked his customary magic in designing the book. David Moore, executor of the Estate of Marianne Moore, has my thanks for his permission to quote from unpublished Moore family letters, and to reproduce Moore's sketches. Elizabeth Gregory and Karen Schoenewaldt, at the Rosenbach Museum and Library, made finding that material a pleasure.

Every editor should be as lucky as I was to have Linda Leavell simultaneously working on a biography of her subject; for conversations about Moore matters large and small, I am indebted to her. As ever, Fred Whiting's timely reading of the introduction re-shaped it for the better, and Emily Wittman's saved it from a number of inelegances. Ellen Levy, whose mind enchants everything to which it attends, knows how much my work on Moore, and I, depend on that attention. As for Luke Carson, I would thank him if it made any sense for warp to thank woof.

I owe a great deal of the making of this book to Elizabeth Wade. She read (and often as not corrected) every word; the best ideas about its assembly were hers. I can only just bear to give her back to her own work, so important has she been to mine.

The Child Development and Research Center at the University of Alabama continues to make my writing life possible. My children, Ingrid, Xander, and Zeke, continue to make the rest of my life a joy. Randy Fowler is the best husband in the world; thank goodness he is mine. Our family, Julie, John, Jack, Conrad, and Jones, make our lives full, and my sister Kelly keeps us all loved.

This book is dedicated with love to Stuart and Liza White, with whom I had tenure before I ever wrote a word.

INTRODUCTION

1. MARIANNE MOORE, 1936–1941

The period examined in this volume, 1936 to 1941, is demarcated by the publication of two of Marianne Moore's books: the fine press limited edition *The Pangolin and Other Verse*, published by her friend Bryher's Brendin Publishing Co. in 1936,[1] and the trade publication *What Are Years*, published by Macmillan in 1941. Its title, *Adversity and Grace*, comes from the poem "The Pangolin," which appears in both books. In that poem Moore describes the eponymous "armored animal" as having the "frictionless creep of a thing/made graceful by adversities" (ll.80–81). Although she could not have known it at the time that she wrote the poem, the late 1930s and early 1940s would be a time of multifarious personal and professional adversity for Moore herself, as well as one in which she came to believe that America as a nation was in need of a grace to which her art had not, until that point, been sufficiently attuned. The concepts she associated with that grace, such as workmanship, permanence, patience, loyalty, and self-effacement, are not by their nature exciting, and the poems she wrote in order to espouse them were received without enthusiasm by many of the periodicals to which she sent them, as well as by many of the critics who later wrote about them. For these reasons this period in her work has not been studied in depth, or, by and large, considered a discrete and significant "period" at all.

My choice to treat it as such arises from my belief that it is in fact a uniquely rich period for readers interested in understanding Moore's most characteristic practices as a poet, including most especially her never-ending process of revision. A significant number of the poems in *What Are Years* are heavily revised versions of poems she originally published in the 1930s. In looking carefully at those revisions, I will suggest, we can see two things: first, the beginnings of the major redaction of her canon most spectacularly in evidence in her 1967 *Complete Poems*; second, evidence of the changes to the aims and methods of her poems that world events, and events in her own home, conspired to make permanent. Something of the nature of that latter change may be seen in the title poem of 1941's *What Are Years*. While in 1936 she chose the impenetrably protected pangolin, "another armored animal" (l.1), to represent a moral ideal, by 1941 she titled her book for a poem in which she is blunt about the impossibility of such protection: "all are naked, none is safe" (l.2–3).

A few biographical details are necessary to know in order to understand her changed attitude, and to begin examining her revised poems in detail. Throughout the late thirties Moore and her mother, Mary Warner Moore, endured lengthy illnesses,[2] and Moore experienced increasing doubts about the value of her own poetry in the face of the rise of fascism in Europe and the advent of the Second World War.[3] As I noted above, the talismanic poem for the period is "What Are Years?" which gave its title to the first trade edition of her poems since 1935's *Selected Poems*. This poem represented the culmination of (by Moore's own account) a decade's worth of thought about the citizen-artist's aesthetic and moral responsibilities, and has figured ever since in critical accounts of the change in her poetry from its heights of experiment and complexity to its later didacticism. In 1939, however, it was rejected by both the *New Yorker* and the *Atlantic Monthly*. "What Are Years?" also appears in its entirety as the work of Moore's fictional avatar in her never-published novel *The Way We Live Now*. Moore spent much of the middle and late 1930s at work on the novel, about which even her closest friends knew nothing; her work was brought to a close by Macmillan's rejection of it in 1940. In 1941, moreover, *Selected Poems*, her best known book, was remaindered as she was preparing *What Are Years*. Moore met her professional disappointments with equanimity, but the consistency of those disappointments speaks to a change both in Moore's work and in her vision of the audience she was seeking for it. In 1936 Moore was a respected and sought-after contributor to artistically prestigious journals such as *Poetry*, *Criterion*, and *Life and Letters Today*, and had books in print in both trade and limited edition format. In 1941, she struggled to publish in more generalist periodicals with a wider circulation and a broader audience, and owed the trade publication of her book to a personal sense of indebtedness on the part of Harold Latham, the editor at Macmillan who rejected her novel.[4]

In retrospect, it is in fact remarkable that the poems of *What Are Years* were all written during the same decade, considering the stark differences in theme and style that characterize those written before 1936 and those written between 1939 and 1941. While it is a scholarly convenience to think of a poet's work, and life, in terms of decades, *What Are Years* shows that this convention has the potential to obscure critical turning points in a poet's artistic development. Perhaps most importantly, to think of *What Are Years* as simply Moore's next trade edition of poems after 1935's *Selected Poems* is to miss another way of seeing it: as Moore's first book of poems after a four-year hiatus in her poetry publication. That hiatus began in 1936 after the publication of "Walking-Sticks and Paperweights and

Watermarks" in *Poetry*, and ended in 1940 with the publication of "Four Quartz Crystal Clocks," "What Are Years?," and "A Glass-Ribbed Nest" in the *Kenyon Review*. Scholars have recognized the significance of a previous such hiatus, between 1925 and 1932, which coincided with her editorship of the *Dial*. When she returned after that period to poetry publication, with "Part of a Novel, Part of a Poem, Part of a Play" in 1932, her poems were different from what they had been before, and marked a distinct evolution in her style and sense of audience. I argue here that that the impact of the four-year poetic silence that began in 1936, as evidenced by those poems first published in 1940 and 1941, was as significant; the fact that it is not a commonplace of Moore criticism to discuss it as such is a testament to how carefully Moore structured *What Are Years* to obscure it.[5]

In my view the interest of *What Are Years* as a milestone in Moore's writing is twofold. First, it is the meeting point between the end of the early Moore and the beginning of the late, the book in which one can read a decisive turn away from polysemous complexity in favor of didactic simplicity. Second, as I suggested earlier, it is the first book in which Moore makes thoroughgoing revisions to major poems with the intention of re-shaping her earlier work to fit later intentions. This second point is crucial. Accounts of Moore's revisionary practices, and the differences between her early and late styles they reflect, have focused on 1951's *Collected Poems*, and 1967's *Complete Poems*. There are good reasons for that choice: those two volumes, the latter in particular, are, as Moore intended them to be, showcases for the excisions and revisions that continue to define our understanding of Moore's work. Andrew Kappel's 1991 article "Complete with Omissions: The Text of Marianne Moore's *Complete Poems*" remains the best overview of Moore's ever-deepening commitment to revision, a commitment almost invariably expressed, as he shows, by contraction. Kappel identifies 1951 as a pivotal moment in Moore's revisionary work, arguing that "no awareness of her predilection to pare her work away in reprinting could prepare one for the deep cuts she made at this point" (138). In examining those cuts he writes "the material Moore cuts from her poems when assembling them for her *Collected* is always material of the same sort [:]...passages given over to the detailed presentation of particularities.... [She] always more or less shift[s] the balance away from particularity and toward generalization" (141). As indebted as I am to Kappel's work on Moore's editorial practices, I will suggest here that his emphasis on *Collected Poems* as the site of an unprecedented change is misplaced. The excisions of the kind he describes in relation to "particularities" are abundantly, and systematically, in evidence in *What Are Years*, making it clear that Moore's work in 1951 was not (or not simply) the result of the unique catastrophe of her mother's 1947 death, as Kappel proposes, but the consolidation of a shift begun years before.

2. THE WAY WE LIVE NOW

One place to begin the story of that shift is in the suspension of Moore's poetry writing between 1936 and 1939.[6] As was the case when she stopped writing poetry during the late 1920s, she turned, in the middle to late 1930s, to prose. In 1933 Moore had answered Harold Latham's request that she send him a book of poetry to publish by saying that while she had nothing ready in that line,

> procedure that has seemed to me plausible, would be to mature a piece of fiction I have been reverting to during the last five years and see if it could be published.... I have had a superstitious objection to allowing anyone to know of my preoccupation with the fiction. My mother and brother only, are in my confidence. Aside from them you are the only one to whom I care to give a hint of the matter. However little import the work might have for the public, it would be fatal to me in the treatment of it to be conscious of being watched. I burden you with this confidence because of the strong impression I received in 1921 that you thought I could write a piece of fiction. I have been rather faithful to this ghost since 1929, the year *The Dial* was discontinued, yet see no nearer hope of its coming to light, so in mentioning it I do not feel that I am doing you a favor. I resisted the natural impulse to speak of it, other times when you were hospitable, for how could I know it would ever exist? The vapidly theatrical forecast of other people's novels always seemed to me unlucky;—at least to have a tinge of irony.[7]

Latham responded enthusiastically to the idea of a novel, assuring her that "I value your confidence in telling me about the fiction. Believe me it will be respected. To say that I am eager to have you complete the work, and to see it, is putting it mildly. The day that the manuscript of your novel comes to my hands I shall drop everything to read it."[8] The 1921 exchange to which Moore refers occurred when Moore contacted him about publishing work by Moore's friend and supporter Bryher.[9] While Latham declined to publish Bryher he encouraged Moore herself to try writing fiction. By the time of her letter in 1933 Moore was working steadily on a novel, and would devote increasing time to it as the thirties progressed. The manuscript in question, which came to be titled *The Way We Live Now*, is a novel of three hundred and fifty-two pages, divided into thirty chapters. One measure of the intensity of Moore's work on this project in the late thirties is the sharp drop-off in her publication between 1937 and 1939. In 1936 she published four new poems, her book *The Pangolin and Other Verse*, and nine pieces of prose in periodicals, most of them book reviews. In 1937, she published only four pieces of prose, one of them a chapter (called "The Farm

Show") from the novel. In 1938 and 1939 she published no writing at all. This silence had a number of contributing factors, including most particularly the ill-health of Moore and her mother to which I alluded earlier, but it also testifies to her resolve to see the novel through to completion. She eventually did so, sending the manuscript to Macmillan late in 1939, having received all along encouragement and help from her mother and her brother John Warner Moore (called Warner). In early 1940, Latham wrote to her with bad news:

> I am more sorry than I can say that I must write you that we are not going to make you an offer on your novel.... As I promised you in my earlier notes, we came to this manuscript, which we have so long looked forward to seeing, with far more than ordinary interest and sympathy. Our people have gone over it and I have gone over it. We realize the very considerable standing and reputation you have made for yourself, just as we realize our own pride at being your publishers. We simply did not feel, however, that your novel is one which we could publish with confidence and enthusiasm in the very difficult conditions surrounding us today. In happier times it would have been a nice book to do—a poet's novel and one which would have been treated with respect.[10]

Moore took the rejection with somewhat tenuous good cheer, writing to her brother:

> I am very much pleased with the letter (enclosed) from Mr. Latham. Bear [Moore's mother] has the feeling he would like to have took the story. Anyhow, a doubt would kill our comfort in the matter. If the company had no hope of sales, they couldn't enjoin their salesmen to say "this is a big event." And we're safe and free. (How is my answer? psychologically.) (*Selected Letters* 395–6)[11]

Despite a few suggestions later in her correspondence that she is still thinking about ways to revise the novel, nothing more came of it; it remains in her archive at the Rosenbach Museum and Library in Philadelphia, unpublished by virtue of a specific instruction in her will.[12] Describing a Moore novel is little easier than describing a Moore poem, but generally speaking *The Way We Live Now* centers on Eloise Osgood, a painter and aspiring poet, and her two suitors Alec Van Wart (stalwart member of Eloise's extended family in her home town) and Nicholas Camelford (suave habitué of Greenwich Village). Eloise is initially drawn to Camelford, but eventually finds him shallow: at an important juncture she is troubled by his showing insufficient reverence when John Bunyan is mentioned in conversation. As even this small incident might suggest, the reader of *The Way We Live Now* is not likely to disagree with Harold Latham's judgment of its probable popularity. Surely there were not, in the 1930s, many readers outside of the Moore household who took it as a given that *Pilgrim's Progress* is a sacred text, and one's attitude toward it a litmus test of character. Charles Molesworth succinctly assesses the novel's ambitions and limitations:

> Moore was putting into the novel in an explicit way her concerns about what she felt were the delinquent morals of the day.... Taking into account that the major influence was Henry James, it is evident that Moore's concern with social morality and decorum was not something she could translate into a natural sounding fiction. (299)[13]

Molesworth draws his evidence for the first part of his claim from correspondence between Moore and her brother, and both parts are amply borne out by the novel itself. Eloise closely embodies Moore's own moral and political concerns, professing almost verbatim Moore's own concerns about the moral health of her country as it was being, she believed, compromised by Franklin Delano Roosevelt's "relief" program and his pandering to "the porcine self-interest of our country" (*Selected Letters* 253).[14]

As unprepossessing as the novel might have proved to a general readership, there is much in it to engage readers of her poems, as Warner cannily predicted there would be. In one of his numerous letters of encouragement to Moore on the subject of her novel, he instructs Moore to:

> hand it to [Macmillan] as something that has intensely interested you. As something that will be perhaps of interest to them as an exposition of your character, your methods of work, and your critical judgment of literary values and production rather than as a novel the general public might be expected to drop their coffee cups and seize with both hands to read for a thrill or "a good story."
>
> ...
>
> You have a certain place now in American Letters. This work will be of great interest to the literary world, as a silhouette of you, if for no other reasons and there are other excellences in plenty in the work.[15]

A chapter called "The Standard Poets" contains an especially interesting "silhouette" of Moore. In it (on 225–6), Eloise shyly shows Camelford a poem she has been working on called "What Are Years?" Eloise tells Camelford that its third stanza is the most important to her, and the novel prints the poem in full. Camelford pays slight attention to the poem, missing the third stanza altogether and finding what he reads of it too serious to be engaging. The novel's presentation of the first two stanzas is with one exception ("within" for "upon" in the fifth line of the second stanza) identical to the version that appears in *What Are Years*. The third stanza, however, undergoes a number of changes as Moore has Eloise sit down to work on the poem after Camelford leaves. Eloise's work is intriguing. She begins by sketching the rhythmic structure of the stanza, in a numbered list of lines in which the syllables are rendered as long and short feet. She decides that although she is unhappy with her inability to make the metric pattern regular, it cannot be helped, and turns instead to considering how the punctuation marks effect abrupt changes in the rhythm and tone of the sentences, deciding after some deliberation to insert a comma and change the ordering of a phrase. Her work comes to an end in frustration, however, as she puts the poem away and reflects that perhaps no version of the stanza is finally the correct one.

This passage (on 227–8 of the manuscript) is the only example I know of Moore's demonstrating a thought process behind revision in any detail. Presented as it is in a work of fiction, its relation to Moore's own practices is a matter of speculation. I present it here, on the basis of just such speculation (bolstered by Warner's reading of it in the same way), for three reasons. First, its status as the only piece of writing the novel attributes to Eloise suggests the poem's importance to Moore more generally. Other lines and images from Moore poems are scattered throughout the manuscript, but "What Are Years?" is the only complete poem it includes.[16] Second, Eloise's attitude toward Camelford's lack of interest suggests that Moore anticipated the lack of enthusiasm her new poems initially generated, and was nevertheless prepared to stand by her sense of their moral importance. In revising the poem after Camelford disparages it, for example, she does nothing to make it less serious, but reflects instead that Camelford himself may simply not be a good reader of philosophical content.[17] Third, and most importantly as a caveat to my ensuing discussion of Moore's revisions, the scene of Eloise at work on revising the poem makes manifest what the variant tables I have compiled here and elsewhere imply: that what may look to a reader like matters of minor importance, such as the insertion or deletion of a comma, or the alteration of unrhymed syllables, were of constant and deep importance to Moore as she worked and re-worked her poems. The record of minute and continual alterations to her poems clearly suggests that Moore, like Eloise, was at least as concerned with changes to rhythm and tone as she was with large-scale adjustments and re-fashionings.

It is tempting, and I have not in what follows resisted the temptation, to discuss Moore's revisions mainly with regard to her clear changes of mind about their denotative content. Taken as a whole, however, the variant table for any given Moore poem will often show that her most consistent work was at a finer level, on much subtler points of emphasis and inflection. Eloise's preoccupation with the length of syllables and the potential harmfulness of punctuation ought to function as a caution to Moore's readers, and certainly to her editor, to move ever more carefully in creating a story about what her revisions tell us about her values as a poet. A Moore poem invites its audience to expend on it the same patience Moore brought to every part of its making, not excluding colons, hyphens, and all other markings that go toward creating the "written tone of voice" to which Moore aspired, and which she described as "that intonation in which the accents which are responsible for it are so unequivocal as to persist, no matter under what circumstances they are read or by whom they are read" (*Collected Prose* 32).

3. REVISING THE POEMS

A reading of Moore's revisions for *What Are Years* begins with its table of contents, because the ordering of the poems itself is part of the process by which Moore re-shaped her earlier work. Like *Selected Poems*, *What Are Years* is deliberately achronological in its ordering of poems, placing the most recently published work first. It then collects those poems Moore published in the thirties but did not include in *Selected Poems*, including all of the poems in the "Old Dominion" series, before returning to a group of newer poems. The exception in this final group is "The Pangolin," which Moore (significantly) placed as the penultimate poem in the book. The table of contents might be annotated as follows:

Published in 1940–1941:	What Are Years?
	Rigorists
	Light is Speech
	He "Digesteth Harde Yron"
Published in 1932–1936:	Walking-Sticks and Paper-Weights and Water Marks
	The Student
	Half Deity
	Smooth Gnarled Crape Myrtle
	Bird-Witted
	Virginia Britannia
	See in the Midst of Fair Leaves
Published in 1940–1941:	Spenser's Ireland
	Four Quartz Crystal Clocks
Published in 1936:	The Pangolin
Published in 1940:	The Paper Nautilus[18]

Moore did not consult with T.S. Eliot about the ordering of the poems for this book, but the influence of his method in *Selected Poems* seems to me evident: Moore shaped *What Are Years* so that the principles of her latest work, directness of statement, clarity of focus, and unambiguous moral guidance, would be established first and color the reader's understanding of the whole.[19] To this end she surrounds her earlier, more difficult poems with her later, more accommodating ones. Even her otherwise anomalous placement of "The Pangolin" toward the end of the book serves this purpose, making it clear that the nocturnal, masculine, engineering pangolin has been superseded as Moore's ideal by the nurturing female paper nautilus.[20] Her method in the table of contents is notably effective in obscuring the differences between the poems of the early and mid thirties, and those of the late thirties and early forties. A chronological ordering of the poems would make it difficult to miss, for example, the radical shift from the "difficulty...ordained to check poltroons" of even the revised "Walking-Sticks and Paper-Weights and Water Marks," and the lucid exposition of "Rigorists." It is surprising that the same poet wrote both poems, let alone that they occur in the same book.

One might argue that the same poet did not write them. It is clear at least that Moore in 1941 had a new vision for her long poems of the mid thirties, and that she did what she could in revising them to transform them into poems of the early forties. While Moore rarely reprinted a poem without altering it, however slightly, the scale of her revisions to the long poems of *What Are Years* is new in her work up until that point. Of the seven poems from the mid thirties collected there, three of them ("The Student," "Half Deity," and "Walking-Sticks") are altered so extensively from their earlier versions as to require side-by-side presentations to present all the variants and, thus, might justifiably be called new poems under old names. A fourth, "Virginia Britannia," is likewise transformed by its substantially different final stanza. The aesthetic consequences of Moore's revisions, and the relative value of her work before 1936 and after 1939, are subject to debate. In the 1980s two schools of thought on the subject were articulated most succinctly by John Slatin, who reads Moore's work in the 1940s as a "decline" into a "simplifying, moralizing tendency" (13–4), and Margaret Holley, who finds in it "a new voice and texture" that "embod[ies] aesthetic heroism...openly and...movingly" (112). My own partiality to Slatin's view will become clear. However, the principle aim of this edition is to make those revisions easily accessibly to readers in the hope that others will read them in ways I have yet even to imagine; so much the better if they prove more persuasive than my readings. I hope that one way to begin such an engagement is an account, however partial in every sense of the word, of some of the specific features of her poems on which Moore focused in revising them.

Moore's daily diary for 1941 shows her to have been revising the longer poems of the mid-thirties for inclusion in *What Are Years* during most of February of that year. In January the Poetry Society of America gave Moore its Shelley Memorial Award, then as now an award of money given to "a living American poet with reference to his or her genius and need."[21] On January 21, 1941 Moore wrote to Warner "I feel kind o'active as the result of my Award!" (*Selected Letters* 410) and in a letter dated April of that year she tells Bryher that it was her receipt of the award that suggested to Macmillan that it was time for a book of her poetry. By June her correspondence with Macmillan shows her finalizing the details of the book's title page and cover. Moore, then, made momentous changes to the book's longest poems in a period of months, at the same time that new poems were appearing in print in periodicals, only to be themselves revised for inclusion in the book. As might be expected, the changes she made to the newest poems are matters, for the most part, of punctuation and the correction of printing errors. The changes to the longer, earlier poems are quite different.

Two small but rich examples with which to begin describing that difference occur in lines nine and ninety-seven of "The Pangolin."[22] While Moore did not make extensive changes to the poem in reprinting it, the two I cite here are representative of the large-scale shifts she made elsewhere. First: in the 1936 "Pangolin" lines five through nine consist of a sentence that begins with the promise of a declarative and ends with a surprise interrogative:

> This near artichoke
>   with head and legs and grit-equipped giz-
>   zard, the night miniature artist-
>   engineer, is   Leonardo's
>   indubitable son?

In 1941 the question mark is replaced by a period. What is lost in the change is a kind of playfulness, in both the effect of a line ended with the unexpected uplilt of a question, and in the mental lineage the poet asks the reader to imagine in accepting that a pangolin might be the child of a man. The playfulness of the question reflects back on the word "indubitable," infusing it with the very doubt the word sought to dispel. The question mark invites the reader to inhabit a double consciousness, however momentary. On the one hand, we are permitted to wonder at the comparison (Leonardo had a pangolin baby that looked like an artichoke? Can that really be right?), and on the other led to admire the strangeness of its logic (they are both engineers and artists, after all). Turning the sentence into a statement of fact encourages the reader to set immediately to considering the statement's plausibility, a plausibility most easily established by focusing less on the physical particulars of the image than on its function as a spiritual symbol: the pangolin is Leonardo's "son" by virtue of their shared skill and the poet's admiration of both.

In asserting these differences I am pointing out only what Moore herself was explicit about desiring to achieve. In the same letter to Warner in which she writes about feeling "active" she describes that activity chiefly as an invigorated resolution to "rekkonize my trouble, as being too oblique & obscure" (*Selected Letters* 410). The second example of a change made to "The Pangolin" demonstrates the depth of that resolution by showing the extraordinary linguistic felicity she was willing to forgo in order to pursue it. Lines ninety-seven through one hundred and one compare the pangolin to a sailboat, and are the pivot-point at which the poem stops describing the pangolin and begins describing man. In 1936 those lines appear as follows:

> A sailboat
> was the first machine. The manis, made
>   for moving quietly also,
>   is neither a prisoner
> nor a god; on hind feet plantigrade,
>   with certain postures of a
>   man.

In 1941 they say:

> A sailboat
>
> was the first machine. Pangolins, made
>   for moving quietly also,
>   are models of exactness,
> on four legs; or hind feet plantigrade
>   with certain postures of a
>   man.

There is much to be said about the move from ambiguity to exemplarity in the change from "neither a prisoner/nor a god" to "models of exactness," but the revision that strikes me as most important in these lines is the elimination of "the manis" in favor of "pangolins." That "manis," a word that visually resolves so easily into "man is," should be a synonym for "pangolin" is a coincidence almost too good to be believed in the context of a poem about the deep kinship between the two animals. It is the sort of coincidence that might have given rise to the poem in the first place. I have no evidence that it did, but the word's layers of lexical play are evidently not lost on Moore who uses it in 1936 as the hinge between the poem's description of what a pangolin is and its speculation on what that might tell us about what a man is. It is the single moment in the poem where man and pangolin meet and merge in both significance and sign.

Replacing it with "pangolins" diffuses that moment across the body of the sentence. In the 1941 lines pangolin and man do not meet, even in pun; their only link is an occasional similarity of posture. The effect on the theme of the poem as a whole may be slight, but Moore's decision to remove the word "manis" suggests deeper calculations. It may reasonably be supposed to have saved many readers an extra trip to the dictionary, for example; it almost certainly allows a faster reading of the line, and encourages a reading that concentrates on denotation and content rather than connotation and surface. Depending on the reader's expectations of Moore's poetry such changes might bespeak an "advance" to "profound simplicities" (115) by a poet "at the height of her power" (112), as Laurence Stapleton argues, or "a retreat from the rigorous complexity of her earlier work" (254) by a poet whose "confidence in [the reader's] capacity for response has very nearly vanished" (213), as does Slatin. However one reads them, the effects of the removal of the word "manis," which removes from the poem an unfamiliar word, a piece of vocabulary of use to specialists, a pun, and a localized point at which images in the poem both meet and diverge, are consistent with the effects of Moore's large-scale revisions of her other poems from the early thirties.

No poem shows the range of those effects more dramatically than "The Student." Moore originally published "The Student" in *Poetry*, in 1932, as the "poem" part of the sequence "Part of a Novel, Part of a Poem, Part of a Play" that marked Moore's return to poetry publication after editing the *Dial*. The "novel" and "play" parts were "The Steeple-Jack" and "The Hero" respectively. Moore chose to reprint those latter two poems in her 1935 *Selected Poems*, placing "The Steeple-Jack" first in the volume, where it became the cornerstone of Moore's reputation as a major artist (see Kappel, "Presenting"). "The Student," however, did not reappear until 1941, when Moore reprinted a version so shortened and revised as to render the 1932 poem effectively lost. The 1941 version is the one that is today universally cited, on the rare occasions that the poem is discussed at all. The loss of the 1932 version is a major loss to the Moore canon, both for the sake of its own complex beauty, and for the sake of a coherent story of Moore's development as a poet. While one could argue (and I would heartily agree) that there are other major lost Moore poems ("Pigeons" and "Walking-Sticks and Paperweights and Watermarks," for example) "The Student" is unique in the prominence of its first publication, which made its nine-year disappearance the more perplexing, and in the comprehensiveness with which the revised version effaced, rather than merely superseded, the original.

As in my discussion of "The Pangolin" I will concentrate on several small but exemplary revisions to illustrate the differences between the earlier and the later poem. Moore begins the 1941 version by removing from its first stanza an ambiguity at play in the 1932 version. In 1932 lines four and five of the poem say of the American attitude toward college: "five kinds of superiority//might be unattainable by all, but one degree is not too much." The revised lines in the 1941 version report that "We do incline to feel/that although it may be unnecessary//to know fifteen languages,/one degree is not too much." In the first version there is a relationship between the words "kind" and "degree" in respect to the idea of "superiority," as "degree of superiority" is as colloquial a phrase as "kind of superiority." Thus, the poem may be read to say that while citizens might not reasonably be expected to be multifariously "superior," one college degree is not too much to ask of them. However, the poem may also imply that even in a democratic nation founded on the principle of equality, one degree "of superiority" is desirable in its students. The ambiguity is important, because it encapsulates the tension between Moore's commitment to a social ideal of equality, and her belief in real differences of intellectual accomplishment, or superiority.[23] In the 1941 version no such alternation of readings, between "college degree" and "degree of superiority" is possible: the substitution of "fifteen languages" for "kinds of superiority" tethers the word "degree" to the idea of certification.

While in this case the effect of a revision may be clear, the potentially more interesting question of Moore's motives in making it remains open. One (unlikely) possibility is that she meant all along for "degree" to signify only the completion of a college education and simply missed the play between it and "superiority." Other, likelier possibilities are that she heard the play in the earlier version and a) had consciously designed it to introduce an ambiguity; b) liked the ambiguity it introduced without exactly intending it; or c) neither intended it nor particularly liked it, but tolerated it for other reasons. A reader interested in deciding between such possibilities will find rich material for argument in the poem's many other changes, all of which tend in the direction of narrowing the reader's potential interpretive range. Most often Moore effects that narrowing, paradoxically, by moving away from the specificity of her references. For example, the 1932 poem cites by name Einstein, Emerson, and Audubon, lists at length the subjects of the student's study, and compares the process of education itself to learning to dance and "turn[ing] as the airport wind-sock turns without an error" (l. 34). In 1941 Einstein is subsumed into "expatriates," Emerson becomes "one in New England," and Audubon disappears altogether along with any description of what the student might study or what that study might feel like. I have characterized these moves away from particular historical and material touch-points as "narrowings" because in my reading they foreclose potentially rich avenues for exploration: the relationship of Einsteinian physics, say, to the "science [that] confers immortality" in line ten of the 1932 version. However, a contrary argument might be made that in removing specifics Moore has widened interpretive options: "expatriates" with views on science could prove as fertile ground for the imagination as Einstein, and the more abstract description does not presume to say what facts the reader needs to know in order to read the poem. Moreover, the names Einstein and Emerson (though not Audubon) are still available to the reader in the notes to *What Are Years*, and, subsequently, to *Collected* and *Complete Poems*.

What is less subject to dispute is that at the same time that Moore's 1941 revisions favor abstraction over particularity, they work consistently and unmistakably to simplify the poems' presentations of heroes and villains, and to accentuate the poet's approval and censure of them. An example of such a change is at work in "The Student," the final stanza of which ends, in 1932, with encouragement to and a challenge for the reader: "anyone who studies will advance./Are we to grow up or not? They are not all college boys in France" (ll. 59–60). In 1941 this stanza is gone, leaving the poem to end instead with a portrait of the morally unassailable student who "renders service when there is/no reward, and is too reclusive for some things to seem to touch/him, not because he has no feeling but because he has so much" (87). If, as I argued earlier, *What Are Years* is a more significant instance than has been properly recognized of Moore's middle- and late- period revisionary practices, it is partly because those practices were applied, as in the case of "The Student," to poems that had never before been collected in book form. With only the ephemeral forms of periodical publications with which to compare them the changed poems of *What Are Years* lose most of their drama, leaving the reader with a deeply slanted vision of Moore's concerns and methods.

The issue is especially acute with respect to "Half Deity" and "Walking-Sticks and Paper-Weights and Water Marks," since their appearance in *What Are Years* is both their first and last in any of the trade books Moore oversaw: the facts of their existence, let alone of their permutations, were in this way made fragile. Those permutations are worth preserving because of the subtlety with which they were made and the starkness with which they demonstrate Moore's increasing unease, as the forties began, with poems that offered less than direct answers to the world's urgent moral questions. Moore's 1941 revisions to "Half Deity" are not more numerous than the revisions she made to it in 1936, when she altered the 1935 periodical version for inclusion in *The Pangolin and Other Verse*. All three versions have the same number of lines, and contain much the same amount of descriptive detail. In each version the poem describes a girl trying to catch a butterfly, and focuses on her frustration when the butterfly chooses to land elsewhere than on her hand. Until 1941 the girl is named "Psyche," and the hand the butterfly chooses belongs to a young man named "Zephyr." The key alteration to the 1941 version is the removal of those names and the consequently muted presence of the Eros and Psyche myth on which the poem was originally based. That muting is evident in the poem's *What Are Years* notes, which reproduce the notes from *The Pangolin and Other Verse* except to omit the latter's reference to the phrase "Zephyr's palm": "Carved Marble Group by Jean Baptiste Boyer (Psyche trying to catch the butterfly held out on Zephyr's palm)" (*A-Quiver* 33). The reference is gone because the phrase is; in 1941 the butterfly lights on "a flower's palm" rather than Zephyr's. In *What Are Years* the poem focuses on an unnamed "nymph" chasing a butterfly; the closest it comes to naming a third party in the chase is a reference, in the final stanzas, to "the/west wind...the zephyr." The nymph, once Psyche herself, is a figure for Moore, the first-person subject amid the "we" who have "stopped to watch the butterfly" and "learned to spare the wingless worm" in the poem's second sentence. Her pursuit of the butterfly is characterized by intensity (her gray eyes turn black, becoming all pupil as she gazes at the insect's face), frustration ("Twig-veined irascible/fastidious stubborn undisciplined/zebra!" she cries in the 1936 version), and the fore-knowledge of failure (the butterfly-bush blue dress she wears will never make her look "nice" enough to tempt "the fiery tiger-horse").

In these qualities the nymph's chase is a caustic commentary on Moore's own practice of observation; the fact that Moore never reprinted the poem after 1941 is consistent with her long-standing tendency to suppress poems that were too explicitly self-portraits.[24] Before abandoning it, however, Moore took care in the 1941 version to strip from the poem both its specific inspiration (the Boyer marble) and its mythic dimension: no longer is the nymph's drama of pursuit and failure overtly resonant with the transgression, loss, exile, and return of Psyche's life with Eros. As in the revision to "The Pangolin" a layer of punning is lost in "Half Deity"'s revision ("psyche" means both "soul" and "butterfly"); as in the 1941 "The Student" references to an earlier text a reader must know or learn in order to more fully read the poem are removed. The stakes of the nymph's drama are altered by these changes. The "moral" of the 1936 "Half Deity" might be summarized as "what you inevitably lose in headlong pursuit of beautiful creatures is a piece of yourself." In the 1941 version the moral is simpler: "butterflies cannot be caught by pursuit." "Butterflies" may still stand for many things in the latter version, of course, and "nymph" still suggests an early stage of insect development that relates the girl to the object of her desire. Desire itself, however, the very crux of Psyche's story, becomes with her name's erasure a weakened element in the poem rather than the force, as it once was, as live as the butterfly's resistance to it.

The diminishment of forces in contention, and a resulting emphasis on foregone conclusions, is a broadly applicable description of the effects of Moore's 1941 revisions. It is most clearly exemplified in her re-writing of 1936's "Walking-

Sticks and Paperweights and Watermarks." Because this poem appeared in print only twice (in *Poetry* and *What Are Years*), and perhaps also because it is long and difficult even by Moore's standards, it is largely forgotten today. That is a shame, and I hope that its inclusion in this edition will contribute to a change in its fortune. A paraphrase of the poem is impossible, but, speaking in barest outline, one can say it is interested in spiritual values such as honesty, sincerity, and patience, and the extent to which they can or cannot be manifested in a variety of hand-made objects that include watermarked rag paper, a glass paperweight, and a wax seal on the back of a letter. Moore's focus in the poem on these ideas and objects clearly exemplifies some of the concepts I claimed in the beginning of this essay as central to her work in this period at large: workmanship and permanence, complexity and simplicity, didacticism and beauty.

Moore's revisions of the poem are as complex as the poem is itself, but a brief discussion of two telling examples may serve as an introduction to the whole and an enticement to further investigation. The first occurs in the 1936 poem's first two stanzas, which find the poet taking a walk in an enchanted forest. The poet is "exhilarated" by a world "so stirringly alive" that "the very stones, have life" (ll. 8–13) At the same time that she registers the pleasure of such a world, however, she notes that its cost is that malign forces otherwise relegated to local legend are enlivened too: "Little/scars on church-bell/tongues put there by the Devil's claws…now as outright murderers and thieves,/thrive openly" (ll. 13–21). In the 1941 version, by contrast, the poet will not concede that anything unworthy may be said to thrive, claiming instead that those church-bell scars "and other forms of negativeness need but/be expressed and visible,/to prove their unauthority" (25).

The finality with which the poet here denies "authority" to destructive forces is mirrored inversely in a second significant revision, in which she bolsters the authority she accords an "able workman" introduced later in the poem. This second revision concerns the maker of a glass paperweight who is, in both versions, "a bold outspoken gentleman, cheer-/ful, plodding, to-/the-point, used to the atmosphere/of work." In 1936 these qualities make him "appropriate to the thought of/permanence" when he remarks "this is my taste, it might not/be another man's." By 1941, however, his boldness, cheer, and plodding dedication to work make him "therefore author of the permanent." This revision elevates the workman's character from that which momentarily intersects with an ideal ("appropriate to") to that from which an ideal quality issues in material form as a matter of course ("therefore author of"). Such an elevation is congruent with Moore's change of emphasis in "The Student" from a process of education ("anyone who studies will advance./Are we to grow up or not?") to an idealized endpoint of that process ("he renders service/when there is no reward"). A reader of the 1936 version of "Walking-Sticks" might wonder whether good workmanship, however admirable, is in itself sufficient to achieve the multi-faceted idea of "permanence" around which the poem circles; a reader of the 1941 version is simply told that it is. This revised estimation of the workman's abilities points to a retreat, in 1941, from the implication of the rhetorical question that ends her 1918 poem "Black Earth": "Will/Depth be depth, thick skin be thick, to one who can see no/Beautiful element of unreason under it?" (*Becoming* 238).

4. VARIANTS

Beautiful or not, there is a particular kind of unreason, or rather counter-reason, to the labor of compiling and reading variant tables in the way I have done in this volume and been doing for this introduction. Variants accrue over time in ways that exceed and escape the poet's reasons, becoming a record of the poem's interaction with the world of typesetters, printers, editors, and readers. A poem, and especially a Moore poem, may be in its writing a collaboration in numerous explicit and implicit ways, but a variant table must be a collaboration, not least among the collaborators being the compiler herself. In asking the reader to consider the implication of "Moore's" variants, then, I am inviting us all to participate in a thought experiment: suppose that insight into Moore's reason as a poet arises from careful attention to a form of writing (maybe the only such form) no poet deliberately undertakes. In compiling variant tables that include variants, like printer's errors, that were not "authorized" by Moore, I have created a record that is partly of Moore's work as a poet, partly of her audiences' experiences as readers, and partly of my own current best ideas as the editor of a print volume. In this sense the poet's work may be said to have given rise to a variety of parallel creations. One such creation, for example, is the interpretation I made above regarding Moore's change of the word "manis" to "Pangolins" in "the Pangolin"; another such creation in this volume responds (on 118) to the same change this way: "97. *POV* The manis | *WAY* Pangolins"; yet another response is embodied in the photographic reproductions of the poem in each of the two books where it was published. However much these parallel creations declare themselves to be and will rightly be evaluated as acts of scholarship, they also feel to me as if they flow from what Lewis Hyde identifies as the "gift" nature of creativity: Moore gives her poems to the reader, and the reader repays her by giving something in turn to other readers. The complex and subterranean economy of gifts was of lively interest to Moore herself, who once wrote to her friend and supporter Bryher, "[I] realize more than ever, that one's debts of gratitude must needs be paid to someone other than the one from whom one receives it…" (*Selected Letters* 359).

Whether such gifts will be themselves adequate is another question. Each creative act on my part as an editor of this volume reflects my sense (by no means unique to me) that the way Moore's poems change over time is a vital element of her oeuvre. Capturing change in a static volume, however, is an inherently contradictory goal, and making it legible for the reader is a multivalent challenge. Variant tables, for example, may be as complete and accurate as it is possible to make them and yet by virtue of their very detail be too forbidding to tempt a reader to look at them closely. This danger is evident in the classroom, where teaching a Moore poem in light of its variants requires both teacher and students to learn to read variant tables while also struggling with poems that require patience and persistence even in any one of their extant forms. Side-by-side presentations make better sense for those poems to which the revisions are particularly extensive, but present their own hurdles: they require the reader to read back and forth between texts, thereby obviating the uninterrupted concentration which is one of reading's chief rewards. A reader would have every reason to grow tired of all this apparatus and ask whether it is not the editor's job to make decisions rather than present options, and facilitate rather than impede texts that are inviting to the eye.[25]

The only persuasive answer to such questions will be the usefulness of this book to its readers, a usefulness that will correlate with (among other things) the reader's understanding of what is "inviting" in the presentation of a poem. By reproducing all of the first presentations in facsimile rather than typeset, for example, this book chooses on the side of historical texture over aesthetic consistency (and the ease of reading that accompanies it). I have made this choice for reasons both pragmatic (typesetting introduces the possibility, if not the inevitability, of misprints) and philosophic: my understanding of Moore's work as inextricably tied to and enriched by a reader's knowledge of its change over time is, in my opinion, better served by emphasis on its material traces than by the de-historicizing and monumentalizing effects of uniform reprinting. These latter effects can be powerful tools in their own right, particularly in staking a claim for the wide cultural significance of a poet's work. For example, T.S. Eliot took full and knowing advantage of them in editing Moore's *Selected Poems*, which was designed specifically to present Moore to England as an already established poet, with a body of work ample and distinguished enough to merit "selection." As successful as *Selected Poems* was in 1935 in confirming and shaping Moore's prestige, however, in later years conventional methods of presenting Moore's work began severely to limit the reader's experience of it, and to sequester from view many of the poems on which her status as an indispensable part of American modernism was founded. They have done this in two ways (though each is a valid editorial choice in its own right): by excluding poems Moore herself excluded, and by choosing to reprint only one version of any given poem. Access to early versions of poems and accounts of their subsequent changes have remained frustratingly absent, both where editorial practices have been clearly articulated and scrupulously applied, as in the 1981 Willis and Driver edition of Moore's *Complete Poems*, and where they have been marred by errors and inconsistencies, as in Grace Schulman's 2003 *The Poems of Marianne Moore*.[26]

Robin Schulze's 2002 *Becoming Marianne Moore* provided a new model for editing Moore's work, one that gave rise to my own 2008 *A-Quiver with Significance*, and the present volume. Although I am myself immensely grateful for *Becoming Marianne Moore*, and to have had the opportunity to follow its example, I nevertheless share with the disgruntled reader I hypothesized above the persistent desire for a single book to which I might turn, as reader, scholar, and teacher of Moore's work, for the full scope of her achievement. I would like to hand it to my students, refer to it in my writing, and read through it in the certainty that what I read is, finally and beyond argument, what Moore wrote. I say "book," though future editions of Moore, and every other writer, seem likely to be electronic. Thus far, efforts to make parts of Moore's archive available on the Internet have been fruitless, but that may change in time, and a web-based edition of Moore's work has exciting possibilities.[27] The capacity of an electronic edition, or archive, to store, organize, and present information, however, would not (as best I can guess) satisfy the desire I am describing, the object of which I will persist in calling a book. Even a generation of readers, already born, at home with electronic media and without the atavistic preference for print I harbor, will have a version of the desire for certainty that "authoritative" print editions have promised: the poem not as it was in different instances, but the poem as it transcendentally "is."[28] I have come to think, however, that until such time as we know what poems are, and have the means to represent them, editions such as this one are worth the effort involved in using them. Certainly my own understanding of and admiration for Moore's labor as a poet have been immeasurably enriched by my own as an editor. I hope this edition will be the means of putting those riches back into circulation.

NOTES

1. "Bryher" was the chosen name of Winifred Ellerman, a British writer and patron of the arts who was a friend, correspondent, and supporter of Moore's throughout their lives. Her journal *Life and Letters Today* published a number of Moore's poems in the 1930s and 40s.
2. Moore's illness is not named in her correspondence, though the fact that she was ill is a consistent topic; her mother suffered from shingles, a facial tic, and a recurrent throat inflammation.
3. See *Selected Letters* 336.
4. Though her work was still in demand at *Life and Letters Today*, which published both "A Glass-Ribbed Nest" and "Rigorists" in 1940.
5. An exception to this rule is John Slatin, who calls Moore's "three-year poetic silence" (he is counting the years between her writing, rather than her publishing) "a profound crisis" (13).
6. It is difficult to prove a negative, but Moore usually recorded everything on which she was at work in her daily diaries; no such notations of poems exist for these years.
7. Marianne Moore to Harold S. Latham, 28 September 1933. At the Rosenbach Museum and Library in Philadelphia, Pennsylvania (hereafter cited as Rosenbach).
8. Harold S. Latham to Moore, 4 October 1933, Rosenbach.
9. One record of this exchange is in a letter of Moore's to Bryher, dated 7 July 1921, in which she describes her conversation with Latham: "He said he thought the writing was uneven—some parts were beautifully written, some seemed hurried. I said that I disapproved of certain parts but that I felt some parts couldn't be improved if you waited a hundred years to publish the book" (*Selected Letters* 165). This letter is fascinating in its own right, as it is also the one in which Moore responded to Bryher for the first time after having received *Poems* (1921), the volume of Moore's work that Bryher and H.D. published without her knowledge.
10. Harold S. Latham to Moore, 15 January 1940, Rosenbach.
11. She included in the letter to her brother a carbon of the letter she sent to Latham. That letter (also dated 20 January 1940) says in part: "Success can be a help; dissatisfaction on the part of those who wish one well, is even more valuable, and as I try to feel, an auspice for growth. I wish very much, however, that I need not for my progress, have put on you the rather stiff task of disappointing me" (Rosenbach). At the bottom of this carbon Warner wrote in pencil "Tops!" and drew his signature pair of paw prints; next to it, in red pencil, is "Fine!" with a flourish of underlining. An example of his paw-print mark may be seen on page 368 of Moore's *Selected Letters*.
12. That same instruction prohibits me from quoting from the novel here. While no paraphrase can adequately substitute for that lack, I have characterized relevant passages as carefully as I can, with an express view to representing the work as a accurately as possible without actually reprinting it.
13. Although I am in agreement with Molesworth's assessment of the novel and its stiltedness, it is always well to remember how deliberate Moore was in achieving her effects, and how unconcerned she was to sound like other people. With respect to "natural sounding" dialogue in particular, there is a pertinent passage from a letter Moore wrote to Bryher (27 July 1921, Rosenbach):

    > Mother's talk—talk-out-of-a-book-talk—sometimes affords me great glee as when a woman said one day in Carlisle, "Pretty day, isn't it Mrs. Moore?" and Mother said, "Truly it is a great and beneficent gift," and didn't realize that she had said anything out of the ordinary until I laughed; while very much at variance with the atmosphere of the moment, this sort of talk is not inept.

14. In a letter to Bryher dated 3 October 1932 she is even more scathing: "America is pestered at present by a man named Franklin D. Roosevelt, as Germany has been with Hitler, but I think Mr. Hoover will 'win,' as our neo-Hitler would put it" (*Selected Letters* 279).
15. John Warner Moore to Moore, 13 December 1939, Rosenbach.

16   Thus, in rejecting the novel Macmillan also effectively rejected Moore's newest and, to her, most important, poem. Seen this way it is notable that Latham's letters to Moore do not even note the presence of a new poem in the manuscript.

17   As ever, she was supported through disappointment by the unstinting faith, in every sense, of her family. Writing to Warner (20 March 1940) regarding the rejection of "Rigorists" and "Four Quartz Crystal Clocks" Moore says "I [can] see why they were rejected and...one has sometimes to take a beating and move on to something better: ...technical virtuosity is not the essential nourishment we need at this time." Warner responded immediately (22 March 1940) with a demurral:

> Well let's not argue with one another!... I might remark, however, that if Christ was far from acceptable in His time, and sneered at with the question "what is truth," how shall anyone expect other treatment, when his or her stock in trade can only be ' [sic] truth in beautiful form! In the end it turns out that the only enduring contribution to mankind of that age was what centered in the obscure Galilean!

Both letters are at the Rosenbach.

18   A further, elegiac annotation might note that missing from this list are two poems from the thirties that Moore chose never to collect ("Old Tiger," written in 1918 and first published in 1932, and "Pigeons," published in 1935) and that three of the poems ("Walking-Sticks," "Half Deity," and "See in the Midst of Fair Leaves") disappeared altogether when Moore reprinted *What Are Years* in her *Collected* and *Complete Poems*.

19   Andrew Kappel's analysis of Eliot's work on *Selected Poems*, and the lasting influence of that work on Moore scholarship, is indispensable. See "Presenting Miss Moore, Modernist: T.S. Eliot's Edition of Marianne Moore's *Selected Poems*."

20   I have discussed the significance of this pair of poems elsewhere; see *A-Quiver* xxi-xxii. For a persuasive account of Moore's ordering the poems to make the book a coherent response to World War II, see Slatin 253–8.

21   http://www.poetrysociety.org/psa/awards/frost_and_shelley/

22   The line is erroneously numbered "ninety-eight" in the facsimile reprint in *A-Quiver with Significance*.

23   For an excellent discussion of this issue in Moore's poetry of the 1920s see Redding.

24   Other poems in this category include "Diligence is to Magic as Progress is to Flight" (1915), "To Be Liked By You Would Be a Calamity" (1916), "Holes Bored in a Workbag by the Scissors" (1916), "Roses Only" (1917), "Black Earth" [later titled "Melancthon"] (1918), and "Radical" (1919).

25   Scholars of editing and textual studies generally will recognize that I have just loosely summarized half a century's worth of theoretical debate over and practical experiment in the nature of the editor's work. For an introduction to the history of these arguments in Anglo-American editing and their particular application to Moore's work, see Robin Schulze's "Introduction" to *Becoming Marianne Moore* (1–17).

26   For an analysis of this latter volume's shortcomings, see Schulze, "How Not to Edit."

27   Those possibilities, like many others with regard to the editing of modernist work, were significantly set back in 1998 when U.S. and international copyright regulations were revised so that works published after 1923 do not enter the public domain until seventy years after the death of their author. See Bornstein 41–2.

28   At present the best place I know of to watch at work the crosscurrents of editorial theory, technological innovation, and readerly desire is in the scholarship surrounding the proliferation of editions, electronic and print, of Emily Dickinson's work.

WHAT ARE YEARS
BY MARIANNE MOORE

THE MACMILLAN COMPANY, PUBLISHERS

WHAT ARE YEARS

by MARIANNE MOORE

Author of "Selected Poems," etc.

$1.50

Some of the most individual poetry of recent years has come from the pen of Marianne Moore, and this in spite of her reluctance to have any but the smallest portion of her work published. She has won the praise of the most exacting critics and has caught the attention of all who are concerned with what may have lasting weight, what of our present efforts will influence the poetry of years to come.

Relish, minutely perceived detail, and the precise word, seem able here to convey emotion that is, at times, not the less surprising for having been stirred by an apparently trivial theme.

Miss Moore's new poems are further evidence of her skill in the identifying of form with mood. As T. S. Eliot said of her previous book, some of the poems "have a very wide spread of association. ...Many...are in exact, and sometimes complicated formal patterns, and move with the elegance of a minuet. ... Of the *light* rhyme Miss Moore is the greatest living master."

Following the publication of "Observations" in 1924—her first book to appear in America—she received the Dial Award, and also the Helen Haire Levinson Prize for 1933 and the Shelley Memorial Award for 1940.

What Are Years

WHAT ARE YEARS

THE MACMILLAN COMPANY
NEW YORK · BOSTON · CHICAGO
DALLAS · ATLANTA · SAN FRANCISCO

MACMILLAN AND CO., LIMITED
LONDON · BOMBAY · CALCUTTA
MADRAS · MELBOURNE

THE MACMILLAN COMPANY
OF CANADA, LIMITED
TORONTO

WHAT ARE YEARS

by

MARIANNE MOORE

New York
THE MACMILLAN COMPANY
1941

Copyright, 1941, by
MARIANNE MOORE.

All rights reserved—no part of this book may be reproduced in any form without permission in writing from the publisher, except by a reviewer who wishes to quote brief passages in connection with a review written for inclusion in magazine or newspaper.

FIRST PRINTING.

PRINTED IN THE UNITED STATES OF AMERICA
AMERICAN BOOK—STRATFORD PRESS, INC., NEW YORK

TO
JOHN WARNER MOORE

Certain of these poems first appeared in *Poetry, The New Republic, The New English Weekly, Life and Letters To-Day, Direction, New Directions, The Kenyon Review, Decision,* the *Partisan Review, Furioso.*

Virginia Britannia, Bird-witted, Half Deity, Smooth Gnarled Crape Myrtle, and The Pangolin, were published with the title *The Pangolin and Other Poems* in book form by The Brendin Publishing Company, London, 1936.

CONTENTS

WHAT ARE YEARS?	1
RIGORISTS	2, 47
LIGHT IS SPEECH	4, 47
HE "DIGESTETH HARDE YRON"	6, 48
WALKING-STICKS AND PAPER-WEIGHTS AND WATER MARKS	10, 49
THE STUDENT	15, 50
HALF DEITY	17, 50
SMOOTH GNARLED CRAPE MYRTLE	20, 51
BIRD-WITTED	22, 51
VIRGINIA BRITANNIA	25, 51
SEE IN THE MIDST OF FAIR LEAVES	33, 52
SPENSER'S IRELAND	34, 52
FOUR QUARTZ CRYSTAL CLOCKS	37, 53
THE PANGOLIN	39, 54
THE PAPER NAUTILUS	44
NOTES	47

WHAT ARE YEARS

WHAT ARE YEARS?

    What is our innocence,
what is our guilt? All are
    naked, none is safe. And whence
is courage: the unanswered question,
    the resolute doubt,—
dumbly calling, deafly listening—that
in misfortune, even death,
      encourages others
      and in its defeat, stirs

    the soul to be strong? He
sees deep and is glad, who
    accedes to mortality
and in his imprisonment, rises
upon himself as
the sea in a chasm, struggling to be
free and unable to be,
      in its surrendering
      finds its continuing.

    So he who strongly feels,
behaves. The very bird,
    grown taller as he sings, steels
his form straight up. Though he is captive,
his mighty singing
says, satisfaction is a lowly
thing, how pure a thing is joy.
      This is mortality,
      this is eternity.

I

RIGORISTS

"We saw reindeer
browsing," a friend who'd been in Lapland, said:
"finding their own food; they are adapted

to scant *reino*
or pasture, yet they can run eleven
miles in fifty minutes; the feet spread when

the snow is soft,
and act as snow-shoes. They are rigorists
however handsomely cutwork artists

of Lapland and
Siberia elaborate the trace
or saddle-girth with saw-tooth leather lace.

One looked at us
with its firm face part brown, part white,—a queen
of alpine flowers. Santa Claus' reindeer, seen

at last, had gray-
brown fur, with a neck like edelweiss or
lion's foot,—*leontopodium* more

exactly." And
this candelabrum-headed ornament
for a place where ornaments are scarce, sent

to Alaska,
was a gift preventing the extinction
of the Esquimo. The battle was won

by a quiet man,
Sheldon Jackson, evangel to that race
whose reprieve he read in the reindeer's face.

3

LIGHT IS SPEECH

One can say more of sunlight
   than of speech; but speech
   and light, each
aiding each—when French—
have not disgraced that still un-
extirpated adjective.
Yes light is speech. Free frank
impartial sunlight, moonlight,
starlight, lighthouse light,
   are language. The Creach'h
d'Ouessant light-
house on its defenseless dot of
rock, is the descendant of Voltaire

whose flaming justice reached a
   man already harmed;
   of unarmed
Montaigne whose balance,
maintained despite the bandit's
hardness, lit remorse's saving
spark; of Émile Littré,
philology's determined,
ardent eight-volume
   Hippocrates-charmed
editor. A
man on fire, a scientist of
freedoms, was firm Maximilien

4

      Paul Émile Littré. England
         guarded by the sea,
      we with re-
      enforced Bartholdy's
      Liberty holding up her
      torch beside the port, hear France
      demand, " 'Tell me the truth,
      especially when it is
         unpleasant.' " And we
      cannot but reply,
      "The word France means
      enfranchisement; means one who can
         'animate whoever thinks of her.' "

5

HE "DIGESTETH HARDE YRON"

    Although the aepyornis
    or roc that lived in Madagascar, and
        the moa are extinct,
        the camel-sparrow, linked
    with them in size—the large sparrow
    Xenophon saw walking by
        a stream—was and is
        a symbol of justice.

    This bird watches his chicks with
    a maternal concentration, after
        he has sat on the eggs
        at night six weeks, his legs
    their only weapon of defense.
    He is swifter than a horse;
        he has a foot hard
        as a hoof; the leopard

    is not more suspicious. How
    could he, prized for plumes and eggs and young, used
        even as a riding-
        beast, respect men hiding
    actorlike in ostrich-skins, with
    the right hand making the neck move
        as if alive and
        from a bag the left hand

    strewing grain, that ostriches
    might be decoyed and killed! Yes this is he

whose plume was anciently
the plume of justice; he
whose comic duckling head on its
great neck, revolves with compass-
    needle nervousness,
    when he stands guard, in S-

like foragings as he is
preening the down on his leaden-skinned back.
  The egg piously shown
  as Leda's very own
from which Castor and Pollux hatched,
was an ostrich-egg. And what
    could have been more fit
    for the Chinese lawn it

grazed on, as a gift to an
emperor who admired strange birds, than this
  one who builds his mud-made
  nest in dust yet will wade
in lake or sea till only the
head shows. A nervous restless
    bird that flees at sight
    of danger, he feigns flight

to save his chicks, decoying
his decoyers; never known to hide his
  head in sand, yet lagging
  when he must, and dragging
an as-if-wounded wing. The friend
of hippotigers and wild

                asses, it is as
56   though schooled by them he was

            the best of the unflying
            pegasi, since the Greeks "caught a few wild
                asses but no ostrich;"
60   quadrupedlike bird which
            flies on feet not wings,—his moth-silk
            plumage wilted by his speed;
                mobile wings and tail
64   behaving as a sail.

            Six hundred ostrich-brains served
            at one banquet, the ostrich-plume-tipped tent
68   and desert spear, jewel-
                gorgeous ugly egg-shell
            goblets, eight pairs of ostriches
            in harness, dramatize a
                meaning always missed
72   by the externalist.

            The power of the visible
            is the invisible; as even where
                no tree of freedom grows,
76   so-called brute courage knows.
            Heroism is exhausting, yet
            it contradicts a greed that
                did not wisely spare
80   the harmless solitaire

            or great auk in its grandeur;
            unsolicitude having swallowed up

                    all giant birds but an
84   alert gargantuan
                    little-winged, magnificently
                    speedy running-bird. This one
                        remaining rebel
88   is the sparrow-camel.

WALKING-STICKS AND PAPER-WEIGHTS
AND WATER MARKS

    Jointed against indecision,
    the three legs of the triskelion
        meeting in the
    middle between triangles, run
5   in unison,
        self-assisted. And yet, trudging
        on two legs that move contradictorily,
    despite ghosts and witches, one
9   does not fear to ask for beauty.

    Stepped glass has been made in Ireland;
    they still have blackthorn walking-sticks, and
        flax and linen
    and paper-mills; and reprimand
14   you if you stand
        your stick on such and such a spot.
        You must keep to the path "on account of the
    souls." And all can understand
18   how centralizing loyalty

    shapes matter as a die is hid
    while used; and that such power, unavid
        since secure, can
    mold an at first fluid solid
23   glass weight. Amid
        the wax the seal is safe. Also
        as the water mark's translucence clearly seen
    can fascinate, the vivid-
27   ly white flower attracts one lightly

brushing against sceptre-headed
weeds and daisies swayed by wind. [They said,
    "Do not scatter
your stick, on account of the dead."]
The pathway led
    into woods "where leafy trees meet
    overhead and noise of traffic is unknown"—
the mind exhilarated
        by life all round, so stirringly

alive. Fancy's rude root cudgel
with the bark left on, the woodbine smell-
    ing of the rain,
the very stones had life. Little
scars on churchbell-
    tongues, put there by the Devil's claws,
    and other forms of negativeness need but
be expressed and visible,
        to prove their unauthority.

Patience, with its superlatives,
firmness and loyalty and faith, gives
    intensive fruit.
As a device before it leaves
the wax, receives
    to give, and giving must itself
    receive, "difficulty is ordained to check
poltroons," and courage achieves
        despaired-of ends inversely,—

mute with power and strong with fear.
A bold outspoken gentleman, cheer-
   ful, plodding, to-
the-point, used to the atmosphere
of work, and there-
   fore author of the permanent,
says modestly, "This is my taste, it might not
be another man's." Sincere
      unforced unconscious honesty,

sine cera, can be furthest
from self-defensiveness and nearest;
   as when a seal
without haste, slowly is impressed,
and forms a nest
   on which the raised device reversed,
      shows round. It must have been an able workman,
humorous and self-possessed,
      a liker of solidity,

who gave this greenish Waterford
glass weight with the summit curled down toward
   itself as the
glass grew, the look of tempered sword-
steel; of three-ore-d
   fishscale-burnished antimony-
   lead-and-tin smoky water-drop type-metal
smoothness emery-armored
      against rust. Its subdued glossy

splendor leaps out at the eye as
the light does not shine even from glass
    air-twist canes, or
witchballs. This paperweight, in mass
a stone, surpass-
    ing it in tint, enlarges the
    fine chain-lines on the letter-flap weighted by
its hardened rain-drop surface.
       The paper-mold's similarly

at first unsolid blues, yellow-
whites and lavenders, when seen through, show
    leopards, eagles,
quills, acorns and anvils. "Stones grow,"
as volcano-
    sides and quartz-mines prove. "Plants feel? Men
    think." "Airmail is quick." "Save rags, bones, metals." Hopes
are harvest when deeds follow
    words postmarked "Dig for victory."

Postmark behests are clearer than
the water marks beneath,—than ox, swan,
    crane, or dolphin,
than eastern, open, jewelled, Span-
ish, Umbrian
    crown,—as symbols of endurance.
    And making the envelope secure, the sealed
wax reveals a pelican
    studying affectionately

                    the nest's three-in-one upturned tri-
                    form face. "For those we love, live and die"
                        the motto reads.
                    The pelican's community
113   of throats, the high-
                        way's trivia or crow's-foot where
                        three roads meet, the fugue, the awl-leafed juniper's
                    whorls of three, objectify
117   welded divisiveness. Of the

                    juniper that in balladry
                    has been kept green, the fugue's three times three
                        reiterat-
                    ed chain of interactingly
122   linked harmony,
                        says "On the first day of Christmas
                        my true love he sent unto me, part of a
                    bough of a juniper-tree,"
126   repeated to infinity.

THE STUDENT

"In America," began
the lecturer, "everyone must have a
degree. The French do not think that
all can have it, they don't say everyone
    must go to college." We
do incline to feel
    that although it may be unnecessary

to know fifteen languages,
one degree is not too much. With us, a
school—like the singing tree of which
the leaves were mouths singing in concert—is
    both a tree of knowledge
and of liberty,—
    seen in the unanimity of college

mottoes, *lux et veritas,*
Christo et ecclesiae, sapiet
felici. It may be that we
have not knowledge, just opinions, that we
    are undergraduates,
not students; we know
    we have been told with smiles, by expatriates

of whom we had asked "When will
your experiment be finished?" "Science
is never finished." Secluded
from domestic strife, Jack Bookworm led a
    college life, says Goldsmith;

    and here also as
28 in France or Oxford, study is beset with

    dangers,—with bookworms, mildews,
    and complaisancies. But someone in New
    England has known enough to say
    the student is patience personified,
     is a variety
    of hero, "patient
35 of neglect and of reproach,"—who can "hold by

    himself." You can't beat hens to
    make them lay. Wolf's wool is the best of wool,
    but it cannot be sheared because
    the wolf will not comply. With knowledge as
     with the wolf's surliness,
    the student studies
42 voluntarily, refusing to be less

    than individual. He
    "gives his opinion and then rests on it;"
    he renders service when there is
    no reward, and is too reclusive for
     some things to seem to touch
    him, not because he
49 has no feeling but because he has so much.

16

HALF DEITY

half worm. We all, infant and adult, have
   stopped to watch the butterfly, last of the
   elves, and learned to spare the wingless worm
      that hopefully ascends the tree. What zebra
   could surpass the zebra-
      striped swallow-tail of South America
on whose half-transparent wings, crescents engrave

the silken edge with dragon's blood, weightless?
   They that have wings must not have weights. The north's
   yellower swallow-tail with a pitch-
      fork-scalloped edge, has tails blunter at the tip.
   Flying with droverlike
      tenacity and weary from its trip,
one has lighted on the elm. Its yellowness

that almost counterfeits a leaf's, has just
   now been observed. A nymph approaches, dressed
   in Wedgwood blue, tries to touch it and
      must follow to *micromalus*, the midget
   crab-tree, to a pear-tree,
      and from that, to the flowering pomegranate.
Defeated but encouraged by each new gust

of wind, forced by the summer sun to pant,
   she stands on rug-soft grass; though some are not
   permitted to gaze informally
      on majesty in such a manner as she
   is gazing here. The blind

17

             all-seeing butterfly, afraid of the
28   slight finger, floats as though it were ignorant,

       across the path, and choosing a flower's palm
          of air and stamens, settles; then pawing
          like a horse, turns round,—apostrophe-
             tipped brown antennae porcupining out as
          it arranges nervous
          wings. Aware that curiosity has
35   been pursuing it, it cannot now be calm.

       The butterfly's tobacco-brown unglazed
          china eyes and furry countenance confront
          the nymph's large eyes—gray eyes that now are
             black, for she with controlled agitated glance
          explores the insect's face
          and all's a-quiver with significance.
42   It is Goya's scene of the tame magpie faced

       by crouching cats. Butterflies do not need
          home advice. As though the admiring nymph
          were patent-leather cricket singing
             loud or gnat-catching garden-toad, the swallow-
          tail bewitched and haughty,
          springs away; flies where she cannot follow,
49   trampling the air as it trampled the flowers, feed-

       ing where it pivots. Equine irascible
          unwormlike unteachable butterfly-
          zebra! Sometimes one is grateful to
             a stranger for looking very nice; to the

           friendly outspread hand. But
              it flies, drunken with triviality
56   or guided by visions of strength, off until,

           diminishing like wreckage on the sea,
              rising and falling easily, it mounts
                 the swell and keeping its true course with
                    what swift majesty, indifferent to
              her, is gone. Deaf to ap-
                 proval, magnet-nice as it fluttered through
63   airs now slack now fresh, it had strict ears when the

           west wind spoke; for pleased by the butterfly's
              inconsequential ease, he held no net,
                 did not regard the butterfly-bush
                    as a trap, hid no decoy in half-shut
              palm since his is not a
                 covetous hand. It was not Oberon, but
70   this quietest wind with piano replies,

           the zephyr, whose detachment was enough
              to tempt the fiery tiger-horse to stand,
                 eyes staring skyward and chest arching
                    bravely out—historic metamorphoser
              and saintly animal
                 in India, in Egypt, anywhere.
77   Their talk was as strange as my grandmother's muff.

SMOOTH GNARLED CRAPE MYRTLE

A brass-green bird with grass-
green throat smooth as a nut, springs from
twig to twig askew, copying the
Chinese flower piece,—businesslike atom
in the stiff-leafed tree's blue-
pink dregs-of-wine pyramids
of mathematic
circularity; one of a
pair. A redbird with a hatchet
crest lights straight, on a twig
between the two, bending the
peculiar
bouquet down; and there are

moths and lady-bugs and
a boot-jack firefly with black wings
and pink head. "The legendary white-
eared black bulbul that sings
only in pure Sanskrit" should
be here—"tame clever
true nightingale." The cardinal-
bird that is usually a
pair, looks somewhat odd, like
"the ambassadorial
Inverness
worn by one who dresses

in New York but dreams of
London." It was artifice saw,

> on a patch-box pigeon-egg, room for
> fervent script, and wrote as with a bird's claw
>   under the pair on the
>   hyacinth-blue lid—"joined in
> friendship, crowned by love."
> An aspect may deceive; as the
> elephant's columbine-tubed trunk
>   held waveringly out—
>   an at will heavy thing—is
>   delicate.
>   Art is unfortunate.
>
> One may be a blameless
> bachelor, and it is but a
>   step to Congreve. A Rosalindless
> redbird comes where people are, knowing they
>   have not made a point of
>   being where he is—this bird
> which says not sings, "with-
> out loneliness I should be more
> lonely, so I keep it"—half in
> Japanese. And what of
> our clasped hands that swear, "By Peace
>   Plenty; as
>   by Wisdom Peace." Alas!

BIRD-WITTED

With innocent wide penguin eyes, three
    large fledgling mocking-birds below
the pussy-willow tree,
    stand in a row,
wings touching, feebly solemn,
till they see
        their no longer larger
        mother bringing
something which will partially
feed one of them.

Toward the high-keyed intermittent squeak
    of broken carriage-springs, made by
the three similar, meek-
    coated bird's-eye
freckled forms she comes; and when
from the beak
        of one, the still living
        beetle has dropped
out, she picks it up and puts
it in again.

Standing in the shade till they have dressed
    their thickly-filamented, pale
pussy-willow-surfaced
    coats, they spread tail
and wings, showing one by one,
the modest
        white stripe lengthwise on the
        tail and crosswise

             underneath the wing, and the
30   accordion

             is closed again. What delightful note
                with rapid unexpected flute-
             sounds leaping from the throat
                of the astute
35   grown bird, comes back to one from
             the remote
                    unenergetic sun-
                    lit air before
             the brood was here? Why has the
40   bird's voice become

             harsh? A piebald cat observing them,
                is slowly creeping toward the trim
             trio on the tree-stem.
                Unused to him
45   the three make room—uneasy
             new problem.
                    A dangling foot that missed
                    its grasp, is raised
             and finds the twig on which it
50   planned to perch. The

             parent darting down, nerved by what chills
                the blood, and by hope rewarded—
             of toil—since nothing fills
                squeaking unfed
55   mouths, wages deadly combat,

and half kills
> with bayonet beak and
> cruel wings, the
intellectual cautious-
ly c r e e p ing cat.

VIRGINIA BRITANNIA

Pale sand edges England's Old
Dominion. The air is soft, warm, hot,
    above the cedar-dotted emerald shore
known to the redbird,
    the red-coated musketeer,
    the trumpet-flower, the cavalier,
the parson, and the
    wild parishioner. A deer-
track in a church-floor
brick, and a fine pavement-
tomb with engraved top, remain.
The now tremendous vine-en-
compassed hackberry
    starred with the ivy-flower,
    shades the church tower.
And "a great sinner lyeth here" under
    the sycamore.

A fritillary zigzags
toward the chancel-shaded resting-place
    of this unusual man and sinner who
"waits for a joyful
    resurrection." We-rewo-
    comoco's fur crown could be no
odder than we were,
    with ostrich, Latin motto,
    and small gold horse-shoe,
as arms for an able
sting-ray-hampered pioneer—
painted as a Turk, it seems—

continuously
    exciting Captain Smith
    who, patient with
his inferiors, was a pugnacious
    equal, and to

Powhatan as unflatter-
ing as grateful. Rare Indian, crowned by
    Christopher Newport! The Old Dominion has
all-green grasshoppers
    in all-green box-sculptured grounds.
    An almost English green surrounds
them. Care has formed a-
    mong unEnglish insect sounds,
    the white wall-rose. As
thick as Daniel Boone's grape-
vine, the stem has wide-spaced great
    blunt alternating ostrich-
skin warts that were thorns.
    Care has formed walls of yew
    since Indians knew
the Fort Old Field and narrow neck of land
    that Jamestown was.

Observe the terse Virginian,
the mettlesome gray one that drives the
    owl from tree to tree and imitates the call
of whippoorwill or
    lark or katydid—the lead-
    gray lead-legged mocking-bird with head

held half away, and
　　　　　meditative eye as dead
　　　as sculptured marble
　　eye, alighting noiseless,
　　musing in the semi-sun,
　　standing on tall thin legs as
　　if he did not see,
　　　　　conspicuous, alone,
　　　　　　on the round stone-
　　topped table with lead cupids grouped to form
　　　　the pedestal.

Narrow herring-bone-laid bricks,
a dusty pink beside the dwarf box-
　　bordered pansies, share the ivy-arbor shade
with cemetery
　　　lace settees, one at each side,
　　　and with the bird: box-bordered tidewater gigantic
　　　jet black pansies—splendor; pride—
　　not for a decade
dressed, but for a day, in
overpowering velvet; and
gray-blue-Andalusian-
cock-feather pale ones
　　　ink-lined on the edge, fur-
　　　　eyed, with ochre
on the cheek. The at first slow, saddle-horse
　　quick cavalcade

of buckeye-burnished jumpers
and five-gaited mounts, the work-mule and
   show-mule and witch-cross door and 'strong sweet prison'
are a part of what
   has come about—in the Black
   idiom—from "advancin' back-
wards in a circle;"
   from taking The Potomac
   cowbirdlike, and on
The Chickahominy
establishing the Negro,
inadvertent ally and
best enemy of
      tyranny. Rare unscent-
      ed, provident-
ly hot, too sweet, inconsistent flower-bed!
   Old Dominion

flowers are curious. Some wilt
in daytime and some close at night. Some
   have perfume; some have not. The scarlet much-quilled
fruiting pomegranate,
   the African violet,
      fuchsia and camellia, none; yet
the house-high glistening
   green magnolia's velvet-
   textured flower is filled
with anaesthetic scent
as inconsiderate as
the gardenia's. Even the

gardenia, a-
       gainst dark leaf-vein on green-
       er leaf when seen
against the light, has not near it more small
   bees, than the frilled

silk substanceless faint flower of
the crape-myrtle has. Odd Pamunkey
   princess, birdclaw-earringed; with a pet raccoon
from the Mattapo-
       ni (what a bear!) Feminine
       odd Indian young lady! Odd thin-
gauze-and-taffeta-
       dressed English one! Terrapin
   meat and crested spoon
feed the mistress of French
plum-and-turquoise-piped chaise-longue;
of brass-knobbed slat front-door and
everywhere open
       shaded house on Indian-
       named Virginian
streams in counties named for English lords. The
   rattlesnake soon

said from our once dashingly
undiffident first flag, "don't tread on
   me,"—tactless symbol of a new republic.
Priorities were
       cradled in this region not
       noted for humility; spot

that has high-singing
    frogs, cotton-mouth snakes and cot-
  ton-fields; a unique
Lawrence pottery with
loping wolf design; and too
unvenomous terrapin
in tepid greenness,
    idling near the sea-top;
    tobacco-crop
records on church walls; a Devil's Woodyard;
  and the one-brick-

thick serpentine wall built by
Jefferson. Like strangler figs choking
  a banyan, not an explorer, no impe-
rialist, not one
    of us, in taking what we
    pleased—in colonizing as the
saying is—has been
    a synonym for mercy.
  The redskin with the deer-
fur crown, famous for his
cruelty, is not all brawn
and animality. The
outdoor tea-table,
    the mandolin-shaped big
    and little fig,
the silkworm-mulberry, the French mull dress
  with the Madei-

30

ra-vine-accompanied edge, are
when compared with what the colonists
    found here in Tidewater Virginia, stark
luxuries. The mere
    brown hedge-sparrow, with reckless
    ardor, unable to suppress
his satisfaction
    in man's trustworthy nearness,
    even in the dark
flutes his ecstatic burst
of joy—the caraway-seed-
spotted sparrow perched in the
dew-drenched juniper
    beside the window-ledge;
    this little hedge-
sparrow that wakes up seven minutes soon-
    er than the lark.

The live oak's darkening fila-
gree of undulating boughs, the etched
    solidity of a cypress indivis-
ible from the now
    agèd English hackberry,
    become with lost identity,
part of the ground, as
    sunset flames increasingly
    against the leaf-chis-
selled blackening ridge of green;

                    while clouds, expanding above
199   the town's assertiveness, dwarf
                    it, dwarf arrogance
                            that can misunderstand
                            importance; and
                    are to the child an intimation of
204   what glory is.

SEE IN THE MIDST OF FAIR LEAVES

    and much fruit, the swan—
        one line of the mathematician's
    sign greater-than drawn
        to an apex where the lake is
    met by the weight on it; or an angel
    standing in the sun; how well
        armed, how manly;

    and promenading
        in sloughs of despond, a monster,
    man when human nothing
        more, grown to immaturity,
    punishing debtors, seeking his due as
    an arrow turned inward has
        no chance of peace.

33

SPENSER'S IRELAND

has not altered;—
    the kindest place I've never been,
    the greenest place I've never seen.
Every name is a tune.
Denunciations do not affect
    the culprit;   nor blows, but it
is torture to him to not be spoken to.
They're natural,—
    the coat, like Venus'
mantle lined with stars,
buttoned close at the neck,—the
    sleeves new from disuse.

If in Ireland
    they play the harp backward at need,
    and gather at midday the seed
of the fern, eluding
their "giants all covered with iron," might
    there be fern   seed for unlearn-
ing obduracy and for reinstating
the enchantment?
    Hindered characters
seldom have mothers—
in Irish stories—
    but they all have grandmothers.

It was Irish;
    a match not a marriage was made
    when my great great grandmother'd said

34

                with native genius for
                disunion, "although your suitor be
                        perfection,   one objection
                is enough; he is not
                Irish." Outwitting
                        the fairies, befriending the furies,
                whoever again
                and again says, "I'll never
                        give in," never sees

                that you're not free
                   until you've been made captive by
                   supreme belief,—credulity
                you say? When large dainty
                fingers tremblingly divide the wings
                        of the fly   for mid-July
                with a needle and wrap it with peacock-tail,
                or tie wool and
                        buzzard's wing, their pride,
                like the enchanter's
                is in care, not madness. Con-
                        curring hands divide

                flax for damask
                   that when bleached by Irish weather
                   has the silvered chamois-leather
                water-tightness of a
                skin. Twisted torcs and gold new-moon-shaped
                        lunulae   aren't jewelry
                like the purple-coral fuchsia-tree's. If Eire—
                the guillemot

                                35

             so neat and the hen
          of the heath and the
          linnet spinet-sweet—bespeak
60   relentlessness, then

       they are to me
          like enchanted Earl Gerald who
          changed himself into a stag, to
       a great green-eyed cat of
       the mountain. Discommodity makes
66   them invis   ible; they've dis-
       appeared. The Irish say your trouble is their
       trouble and your
                joy their joy? I wish
       I could believe it;
       I am troubled, I'm dissat-
72   isfied, I'm Irish.

FOUR QUARTZ CRYSTAL CLOCKS

There are four vibrators, the world's exactest clocks;
    and these quartz time-pieces that tell
time intervals to other clocks,
    these worksless clocks work well;
and all four, independently the
    same, are there in the cool Bell
        Laboratory time

vault. Checked by a comparator with Arlington,
    they punctualize the "radio,
cinéma," and "presse,"—a group the
    Giraudoux truth-bureau
of hoped-for accuracy has termed
    "instruments of truth." We know—
        as Jean Giraudoux says

certain Arabs have not heard—that Napoleon
    is dead; that a quartz prism when
the temperature changes, feels
    the change and that the then
electrified alternate edges
    oppositely charged, threaten
        careful timing; so that

this water-clear crystal as the Greeks used to say,
    this "clear ice" must be kept at the
same coolness. Repetition, with
    the scientist, should be
synonymous with accuracy.

37

                The lemur-student can see
28   that an aye-aye is not

            an angwan-tíbo, potto, or loris. The sea-
                side burden should not embarrass
            the bell-buoy with the buoy-ball
                endeavoring to pass
            hotel patronesses; nor could a
                practiced ear confuse the glass
35   eyes for taxidermists

            with eye-glasses from the optometrist. And as
                MEridian-7   1, 2
            1, 2 gives, each fifteenth second
                in the same voice, the new
            data—"The time will be" so and so—
                you realize that "when you
42   hear the signal," you'll be

            hearing Jupiter or jour pater, the day god—
                the salvaged son of Father Time—
            telling the cannibal Chronos
                (eater of his proxime
            newborn progeny) that punctual-
48   ity is not a crime.

38

THE PANGOLIN

Another armored animal—scale
    lapping scale with spruce-cone regu-
      larity until they
form the uninterrupted central
    tail-row. This near artichoke
      with head and legs and grit-equipped giz-
zard, the night miniature artist-
    engineer, is   Leonardo's
      indubitable son. Im-
pressive animal
and toiler, of whom we seldom hear.
    Armor seems extra. But for him,
the closing ear-
    ridge—or bare
    ear lacking even this small
      eminence—and similarly safe

contracting nose and eye apertures
    impenetrably closable,
      are not;—a true ant-eat-
er, not cockroach-eater, who endures
    exhausting solitary
      trips through unfamiliar ground at night,
returning before sunrise; stepping
    in the moonlight,   on the moonlight
      peculiarly, that the out-
    side edges of his
hands may bear the weight and save the claws
    for digging. Serpentined about

                the tree, he draws
                    away from
                    danger unpugnaciously,
                    with no sound but a harmless hiss; keep-

ing the fragile grace of the Thomas-
    of-Leighton-Buzzard Westminster
    Abbey wrought-iron vine, or
rolls himself into a ball that has
    power to defy all effort
        to unroll it;—strongly intailed, neat
        head for core, on neck not breaking off,
            with curled-in feet.   Nevertheless
                he has sting-proof scales; and nest
        of rocks closed with earth
from inside, which he can thus darken.
            Sun and moon and day and night and man and beast
each with a splen-
    dor which man
    in all his vileness cannot
        set aside; each with an excellence!

'Fearful yet to be feared,' the armored
    ant-eater met by the driver
    ant does not turn back, but
engulfs what he can, the flattened sword-
    edged leafpoints on the tail and
        artichoke-set leg and body plates
        quivering violently when it
            retaliates   and swarms on him.
                Compact like the furled fringed frill
on the hat-brim of

           Gargallo's hollow iron head of a
                 matador, he will drop and will
           then walk away
                 unhurt, al-
                 though if unintruded on
                 he cautiously works down the tree, helped

by his tail. The giant-pangolin-
      tail, graceful tool, as prop or hand
      or broom or axe, tipped like
the elephant's trunk with special skin,
      is not lost on this ant and
           stone-swallowing uninjurable
      artichoke which simpletons thought a
           living fable   whom the stones had
                 nourished, whereas ants had done
      so. Pangolins are
   not aggressive animals; between
           dusk and day, they have the not un-
chainlike machine-
      like form and
      frictionless creep of a thing
           made graceful by adversities, con-

versities. To explain grace requires
      a curious hand. If that which
      is at all were not for
ever, why would those who graced the spires
      with animals and gathered
           there to rest, on cold luxurious
           low stone seats——a monk and monk and monk——

41

        between the thus   ingenious roof-
          supports, have slaved to confuse
        grace with a kindly
manner, time in which to pay a debt,
          the cure for sins, a graceful use
of what are yet
    approved stone
    mullions branching out across
    the perpendiculars? A sailboat

was the first machine. Pangolins, made
    for moving quietly also,
    are models of exactness,
on four legs; or hind feet plantigrade
    with certain postures of a
        man. Beneath sun and moon, man slaving
    to make his life more sweet, leaves half the
        flowers worth having,   needing to choose
        wisely how to use the strength;—
a paper-maker
like the wasp; a tractor of food-stuffs,
    like the ant; spidering a length
of web from bluffs
    above a
    stream; in fighting, mechanicked
    like the pangolin; capsizing in

disheartenment. Bedizened or stark
    naked, man, the self, the being
    we call human, writing-

42

    master to this world, griffons a dark
        "Like does not like like that is
           obnoxious;" and writes errror with four
  r's. Among animals, one has a
        sense of humor.   Humor saves a
      few steps, it saves years. Unig-
norant, modest and
unemotional, and all emo-
      tion, he has everlasting vig-
or, power to grow
  though there are
  few creatures who can make one
  breathe faster, and make one erecter.

Not afraid of anything is he
      and then goes cowering forth, tread paced
    to meet an obstacle
at every step. Consistent with the
    formula—warm blood, no gills,
        two pairs of hands and a few hairs—that
    is a mammal; there he sits in his
        own habitat,   serge-clad, strong-shod.
        The prey of fear, he, always
  curtailed, extinguished,
thwarted by the dusk, work partly done,
      says to the alternating blaze,
  "Again the sun!
  anew each
  day; and new and new and new,
  that comes into and steadies my soul."

43

THE PAPER NAUTILUS

For authorities whose hopes
are shaped by mercenaries?
   Writers entrapped by
   teatime fame and by
commuters' comforts? Not for these
   the paper nautilus
   constructs her thin glass shell.

   Giving her perishable
souvenir of hope, a dull
   white outside and smooth-
   edged inner surface
glossy as the sea, the watchful
   maker of it guards it
   day and night; she scarcely

eats until the eggs are hatched.
Buried eight-fold in her eight
   arms, for she is in
   a sense a devil-
fish, her glass ramshorn-cradled freight
   is hid but is not crushed.
   As Hercules, bitten

by a crab loyal to the hydra,
was hindered to succeed,
   the intensively
   watched eggs coming from
the shell free it when they are freed,—

                leaving its wasp-nest flaws
                of white on white, and close-

            laid Ionic chiton-folds
            like the lines in the mane of
                a Parthenon horse,
                round which the arms had
            wound themselves as if they knew love
                is the only fortress
                strong enough to trust to.

A Note on the Notes———

A willingness to satisfy contradictory objections to one's manner of writing, might turn one's work into the donkey that finally found itself being carried by its masters, since some readers suggest that quotation-marks are disruptive of pleasant progress; others, that notes to what should be complete are a pedantry or evidence of an insufficiently realized task. But since in Observations, *and in anything I have written, there have been lines in which the chief interest is borrowed, and I have not yet been able to outgrow this hybrid method of composition, acknowledgments seem only honest. Perhaps those who are annoyed by provisos, detainments, and postscripts, could be persuaded to take probity on faith, the will for the deed, the poem as a self-sufficiency, and disregard the notes.*

M. M.

NOTES

RIGORISTS

Sheldon Jackson (1834–1909). Dr. Jackson felt that to feed the Esquimo at government expense was not advisable, that whales having been almost exterminated, the ocean could not be restocked as a river can be with fish, and having prevailed on the Government to authorize the importing of reindeer from Siberia, he made an expedition during the summer of 1891, procured 16 reindeer—by barter—and later brought others. *Report on Introduction of Domestic Reindeer into Alaska, 1895; 1896; 1897; 1899,* by Sheldon Jackson, General Agent of Education in Alaska. U.S. Educ. Bureau, Washington.

LIGHT IS SPEECH

A man already harmed: Jean Calas, unjustly accused of murdering his son, and put to death, March 9, 1762. In vindicating him and his household, Voltaire "fut le premier que S'éleva en sa faveur. Frapé de l'impossibilité de crime dont acusait Calas le pere, ce fut lûy qui engagea le veuve a venir demander justice au Roy, . . ." *The History of the Misfortunes of John Calas, a Victim to Fanaticism, to which is added a Letter from M. Calas To His Wife and Children; Written by M. De Voltaire.* Printed by P. Williamson. Edinburgh, M, DCC, LXXVI.

Creach'h d'Ouessant aeromaritime lighthouse, the first observable—as planned—by ships and planes approaching the continent from North or South America.

Montaigne, captured by bandits and unexpectedly released, says "I was told that I owed my deliverance to my bearing and the uncowed resoluteness of my speech, which showed that I was too good a fellow to hold up."

47

Littré (1801–1881) devoted the years 1839–1862 to translating and editing Hippocrates.

Bartholdy's Liberty.

"Tell me the truth," etc. Marshal Pétain.

"Animate whoever thinks of her." "Paradise Lost" by Janet Flanner in *Decision,* January, 1941.

HE "DIGESTETH HARDE YRON"

Lyly's *Euphues:* "the estrich digesteth harde yron to preserve his health."

The large sparrow. "Xenophon (Anabasis, I,5,2) reports many ostriches in the desert on the left . . . side of the middle Euphrates, on the way from North Syria to Babylonia." *Animals for Show and Pleasure in Ancient Rome* by George Jennison.

A symbol of justice, men in ostrich-skins, Leda's egg, and other allusions: *Ostrich Egg-shell Cups from Mesopotamia* by Berthold Laufer, The Open Court, May, 1926. "An ostrich plume symbolized truth and justice, and was the emblem of the goddess Ma-at, the patron saint of judges. Her head is adorned with an ostrich feather, her eyes are closed, . . . as Justice is blind-folded."

Six hundred ostrich brains. At a banquet given by Elagabalus. See above; *Animals for Show and Pleasure.*

Egg-shell goblets, e.g., the painted ostrich-egg cup mounted in silver-gilt by Elias Geier of Leipzig about 1589. *Antiques in and About London* by Edward Wenham; *New York Sun,* May 22, 1937.

Eight pairs of ostriches. See above; *Animals for Show and Pleasure.*

Sparrow-camel: στρουθιοκάμηλος.

48

WALKING-STICKS AND PAPER-WEIGHTS AND WATER MARKS

"Where leafy trees meet overhead." Travel page, *New York Sun*.

Little scars on churchbell-tongues. In *Little Known England*, Harold Donald Eberlein quotes John Leland: "there is the spire and choir of Saint Alkmund's where 'in the year 1533, uppon Twelffe daye, in Shrowsburie, the Dyvyll appeared . . . when the Preest was at High Masse, with great tempeste and Darknesse, soe that as he pasyd through, he mounted upp the Steeple in the sayd churche, tering the wyers of the clocke, and put the prynt of his clawes uppon the 4th bell, and tooke one of the pynnacles away with him, and for the Tyme stayde all the Bells in the churches within the sayd Towne, that they could neither toll nor ringe.'"

"Difficulty is ordained to check poltroons." Giordano Bruno.

"Stones grow," etc. Quotation in the *Vest Pocket Manual of Printing;* Inland Printer Co., Chicago.

Water marks: in book paper; oxhead (Van Gelder), swan (1411 and earlier), dolphin (Auvergne and earlier), crown (B. Cramer, Van Gelder, various Dutch papers, Kelmscott), eagle (Basle mill 1633), Umbrian crown (Umbria handmade), anvil (Kelmscott). Machine-made paper: eastern crown (Papyrus Regia), open crown (Eaton's [Berkshire] Souvenir Bond), jeweled crown (Lion Ledger), leopard (Florian); eagle (U. S. Government), quill (Crane's Post), acorn (Whiting).

"For those we love live and die:" motto surrounding pelican and young on an 18th century seal.

The fugue's reiterated chain: exposition, development, conclusion.

"On the first day of Christmas." "The Twelve Presents" in

Welcome Christmas: Legends, Carols, Stories collected by Eleanor Graham (Dutton).

THE STUDENT

"In America." Les Idéals de l'Éducation Française; lecture, December 3, 1931, by M. Auguste Desclos, Director-adjoint, Office National des Universites et Écoles Françaises de Paris.

The singing tree. Each leaf was a mouth, and every leaf joined in concert. *Arabian Nights*.

Lux et veritas (Yale); *Christo et ecclesiae* (Harvard); *sapiet felici,—*

"Science is never finished." Professor Einstein to an American student; *New York Times*.

Jack Bookworm, in Goldsmith's *The Double Transformation*.

A variety of hero: Emerson in *The American Scholar;* "there can be no scholar without the heroic mind;" "let him hold by himself; . . . patient of neglect, patient of reproach."

The wolf. Edmund Burke, November, 1781, in reply to Fox: "there is excellent wool on the back of a wolf and therefore he must be sheared. . . . But will he comply?"

"Gives his opinion." Henry McBride in the *New York Sun*, December 12, 1931: "Dr. Valentiner . . . has the typical reserve of the student. He does not enjoy the active battle of opinion that invariably rages when a decision is announced that can be weighed in great sums of money. He gives his opinion firmly and rests upon that."

HALF DEITY

Swallow-tail of South America. *Papilio filesilans*.
Yellower swallow-tail. *Papilio podalirius*.

50

It is not permitted. Edmund Gilligan: the *New York Sun*, December 1, 1934; *Meeting the Emperor Pu Yi*.

Goya's scene: Don Manuel Osorio De Zuñiga, to the left of three cats, holding in his hand a thread attached to the leg of a magpie.

SMOOTH GNARLED CRAPE MYRTLE

J. I. Lawrence, *New York Sun*, June 23, 1934: "Bulbul is a broadly generic term like sparrow, warbler, bunting. . . . The legendary nightingale of Persia is the white-eared bulbul, *Pycnotus leucotis*, richly garbed in black velvet, trimmed with brown, white, and saffron yellow; and it is a true bulbul; . . . Edward FitzGerald told what Omar meant: that the speech of man changes and coarsens, but the bulbul sings eternally in the 'high-piping Pehlevi,' the pure heroic Sanskrit of the ancient poets."

"Those who sleep in New York, but dream of London." Beau Nash in *The Playbill*, January, 1935.

"Joined in friendship, crowned by love." Battersea box motto.

"Without loneliness." Yoné Noguchi paraphrasing Saigyo. *The (London) Spectator*, February 15, 1935.

"By Peace Plenty By Wisdom Peace," framing horns of plenty and caduceus, above a clasped hands, on the first edition title-page of Lodge's *Rosalynde*.

BIRD-WITTED

Sir Francis Bacon: "If a boy be bird-witted"

VIRGINIA BRITANNIA

Cf. *Travaile into Virginia Britannia* by William Strachey.

A great sinner. Inscription in Jamestown churchyard: "Here

51

lyeth the body of Robert Sherwood who was born in the Parish of Whitechapel near London, a great sinner who waits for a joyful resurrection."

Ostrich and horse-shoe. As crest in Captain John Smith's coat of arms, the ostrich with a horse-shoe in its beak,—i.e., invincible digestion—reiterates the motto, *vincere est vivere*.

Werewocomoco; Powhatan's capitol. Of the Indians of a confederacy of about 30 tribes of Algonquins occupying Tidewater Virginia, Powhatan was war-chief or head werowance. He presented a deer-skin mantle—now in the Ashmolean—to Captain Newport when crowned by him and Captain John Smith.

Strong sweet prison. Of Middle Plantation,—now Williamsburg.

One-brick-thick wall designed by Jefferson: in the grounds of the University of Virginia.

Deer-fur crown. "He (Arahatec) gave our Captaine his Crowne which was of Deare's hayre, Dyed redd." *Travels and Works of Captain John Smith, President of Virginia and Admiral of New England, 1580–1631;* with Introduction by A. G. Bradley. Arber's Reprints.

The lark. The British Empire Naturalists' Association has found that the hedge-sparrow sings seven minutes earlier than the lark.

SEE IN THE MIDST OF FAIR LEAVES

The leaves thereof were fair, and the fruit thereof much. *Daniel,* IV:12.

SPENSER'S IRELAND

Every name is a tune; it is torture; ancient jewelry; your trouble is their trouble: See *Ireland: The Rock Whence I Was Hewn* by Don Byrne; *National Geographic Magazine,* March, 1927.

The sleeves. In Maria Edgeworth—*Castle Rackrent* as edited by Professor Morley—Thady Quirk says, "I wear a long greatcoat. . .; it holds on by a single button round my neck, cloak fashion."

Venus' mantle. Footnote, *Castle Rackrent:* "The cloak, or mantle, as described by Thady is of high antiquity. See Spenser, in his 'View of the State of Ireland.' "

"The sad-yellow-fly, made with the buzzard's wings;" and "the shell-fly, for the middle of July," Maria Edgeworth: *The Absentee.*

The guillemot; the linnet. *Happy Memories of Glengarry* by Denis O'Sullivan.

Earl Gerald. From a lecture by Padraic Colum.

FOUR QUARTZ CRYSTAL CLOCKS

Bell T. leaflet, 1939, *"The World's Most Accurate Clocks:* In the Bell Telephone Laboratories in New York, in a 'time vault' whose temperature is maintained within 1/100 of a degree, at 41° centigrade, are the most accurate clocks in the world—the four quartz crystal clocks. . . . When properly cut and inserted in a suitable circuit, they will control the rate of electric vibration to an accuracy of one part in a million. . . . When you call MEridian 7-1212 for correct time you get it every 15 seconds."

Jean Giraudoux: "Appeler à l'aide d'un camouflage ces instruments fait pour lat vérité qui sont la radio, le cinéma, la presse?" "J'ai traversé voila un an des pays arabes où l'On ignorait encore que Napoleon était mort." *Une allocation readiodiffusée de M. Giraudoux aux Françaises à propos de Sainte Catherine;* the *Figaro*, November, 1939.

The cannibal Chronos. Rhea, mother of Zeus, hid him from

Chronos who "devoured all his children except Jupiter (air), Neptune (water), and Pluto (the grave). These Time cannot consume." Brewer's *Dictionary of Phrase and Fable*.

THE PANGOLIN

The "closing ear-ridge," and certain other detail, from *Pangolins* by Robert T. Hatt; *Natural History*, December, 1935.

Stepping peculiarly. See Lyddeker's *Royal Natural History*.

Thomas of Leighton Buzzard's vine: a fragment of ironwork in Westminster Abbey.

"A sailboat was the first machine." See F. L. Morse,—*Power: Its Application from the 17th Dynasty to the 20th Century*.

What Are Years

FIRST PRESENTATIONS

ABBREVIATIONS

De	*Decision*
Di	*Direction*
Fu	*Furioso*
Ken	*Kenyon Review*
Liv	*Living Age*
Li	*Life and Letters Today*
ND	*New Directions*
NewE	*New English Weekly*
NewR	*New Republic*
PaR	*Partisan Review*
Po	*Poetry*
POV	*The Pangolin and Other Verse*
Sm	*Smoke*
WAY	*What Are Years*

A NOTE ON THE APPARATUS

In assembling the tables of textual variants I have employed the format Robin Schulze invented for the variant tables in *Becoming Marianne Moore*, and which I subsequently adopted in *A-Quiver with Significance*. Each line entry presents the text as it appears in the first presentation, followed by variants in subsequent presentations. Each variant is noted by an abbreviation from the preceding list, re-numbered if the number of total lines changed in revision, and separated from subsequent variants by a vertical dash " | ." I have not distinguished in the variant tables between Moore's revisions and printers' errors. Where [...] appears, it indicates that I have omitted text that appears unchanged within a given variant. In assembling variant tables I have noted all changes to punctuation and spelling, except where such changes follow only from a difference between American and Biritish usage, as in the case of punctuation placed outside or within quotation marks.

in black and white; and one in red
and white says

Danger. The church portico has four fluted
  columns, each a single piece of stone, made
modester by white-wash. This would be a fit haven for
waifs, children, animals, prisoners,
  and presidents who have repaid
sin-driven

senators by not thinking about them. There
  are a school-house, a post-office in a
store, fish-houses, hen-houses, a three-masted schooner on
the stocks. The hero, the student,
  the steeple-jack, each in his way,
is at home.

It could not be dangerous to be living
  in a town like this, of simple people,
who have a steeple-jack placing danger signs by the church
while he is gilding the solid-
  pointed star, which on a steeple
stands for hope.

THE STUDENT

"In America everybody must have a degree," the French
    man

says, "but the French do not think that all can have it;
    they don't
say everyone must go to college." We
4   may feel as he says we do; five kinds of superiority

might be unattainable by all, but one degree is not too
    much.
In each school there is a pair of fruit-trees like that twin
    tree
in every other school: tree-of-knowledge—
8   tree-of-life—each with a label like that of the other
    college:

lux, or *lux et veritas, Christo et ecclesiae, sapiet
felici,* and if science confers immortality,
    these apple-trees should be for everyone.
12   Oriental arbor vitae we say lightly. Yet you pardon

it as when one thinking of the navy does not know not to
    infer
dishonorable discharge from a D. D. It is a
    thoughtful pupil has two thoughts for the word
16   valet; or for bachelor, child, damsel; though no one
    having heard

them used as terms of chivalry would make the mediaeval
    use of
them. Secluded from domestic strife, Jack Bookworm
    led a

[123]

college life says Goldsmith. He might not say
    it of the student who shows interest in the stranger's
        resumé
by asking "when will your experiment be finished, Doctor
        Einstein?"
and is pleased when Doctor Einstein smiles and says
        politely
    "science is never finished." But we're not
hypocrites, we're rustics. The football huddle in the
        vacant lot

is impersonating calculus and physics and military
books; and is gathering the data for genetics. If
    scholarship would profit by it, sixteen
    foot men should be grown; it's for the football men to
        say. We must lean

on their experience. There is vitality in the world of sport.
If it is not the tree of knowledge, it's the tree of life.
    When Audubon adopted us he taught
    us how to dance. It was the great crab-flounder of Mon-
        tana caught

and changed from that which creeps to that which is
        angelic. He taught us how
to turn as the airport wind-sock turns without an error;
    like Alligator, Downpour, Dynamite,
    and Wotan, gliding round the course in a fast neat
        school, with the white

of the eye showing; or as sea-lions keep going round and
   round the
pool. But there is more to learn—the difference between
   cow
  and zebu; lion, tiger; barred and brown
40   owls; horned owls have one ear that opens up and one
      that opens down.

The golden eagle is the one with feathered legs. The
   penguin wing is
ancient, not degenerate. Swordfish are different from
   gars, if one may speak of gars when the big
44   gamehunters are using the fastidious singular—say pig,

and that they have seen camelsparrow, tigerhorse, rat,
   mouse, butterfly,
snake, elephant, fruit-bat, et cet'ra. No fact of science—
   theology or biology—might
48   not as well be known; one does not care to hold opinions
      that fright

could dislocate. Education augments our natural forces
   and
prompts us to extend the machinery of advantage
   to those who are without it. One fitted
52   to be a scholar must have the heroic mind, Emerson said.

The student concentrates and does not like to fight; "gives
   his opinion

firmly and rests on it"—in the manner of the poet;
  is reclusive, and reserved; and has such
56   ways, not because he has no feeling but because he has
      so much.

Boasting provokes jibes, and in this country we've no
    cause to boast; we are
as a nation perhaps, undergraduates not students.
  But anyone who studies will advance.
60   Are we to grow up or not? They are not all college boys
      in France.

THE HERO

Where there is personal liking we go.
  Where the ground is sour; where there are
  weeds of beanstalk height,
  snakes' hyperdermic teeth, or
  the wind brings the "scarebabe voice"
  from the neglected yew set with
  the semi-precious cats' eyes of the owl—
awake, asleep, "raised ears extended to fine points," and so
  on—love won't grow.

We do not like some things and the hero
  doesn't; deviating head-stones
  and uncertainty;
  going where one does not wish
  to go; suffering and not

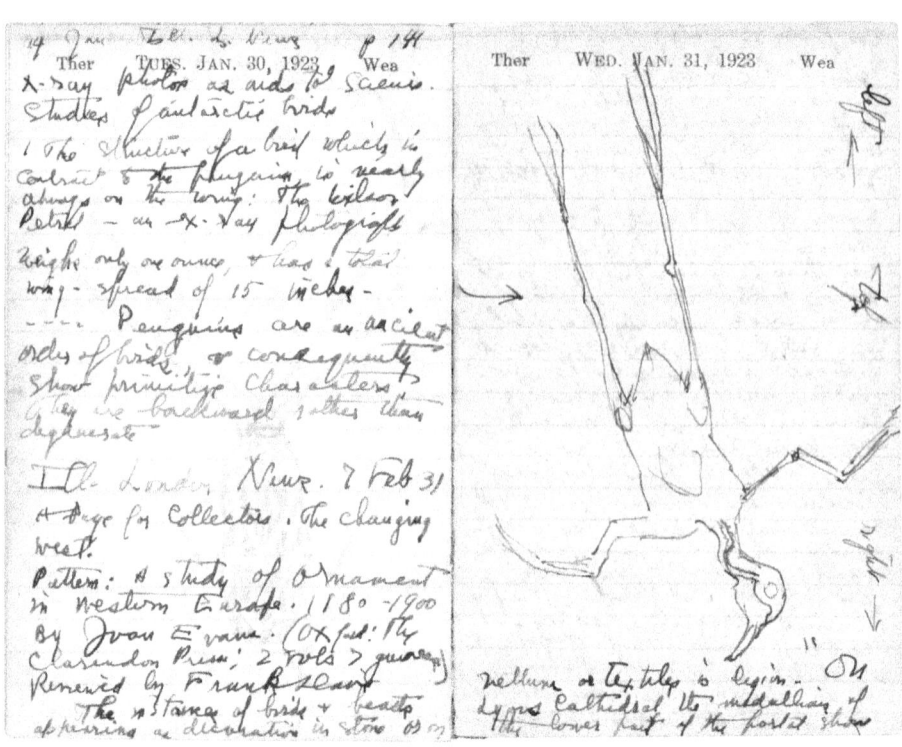

FIGURE 1: "The/penguin wing is/ancient, not degenerate."
"The Student" (1932): ll.41–42.

THE STUDENT

PRESENTATIONS:

Poetry, 40 (June 1932): 122–126.
Furioso, 1 (Summer 1941): 22–23.
What Are Years. New York: Macmillan, 1941: 15–16.

TEXTUAL VARIANTS 1932–1941:

Po Fifteen four-line stanzas, fifty-seven syllables per stanza, with a total of eight hundred fifty-five syllables | *Fu, WAY* Seven five-line stanzas, fifty-seven syllables per stanza, with a total of three hundred and ninety-nine syllables.

ti. *Po* Grouped with "The Steeple-Jack" and "The Hero" under the title "Part of a Novel, Part of a Poem, Part of a Play" | *Fu, WAY* "The Student"

The revisions to this poem between its 1932 and 1941 presentations are too extensive to be enumerated by line; instead I have provided a side-by-side comparison of the presentations in *Poetry* and *What Are Years*, with material unique to each poem marked in bold. Because the variants between the *Furioso* and *What Are Years* presentations are few and minor, I begin with a brief table comparing them.

5. *Fu are* inclined | *WAY* do incline
14. *Fu* opinions; […] undergraduates | *WAY* opinions, […] undergraduates,
15. *Fu* students, as when | *WAY* students; we know
16. *Fu* asked, | *WAY* asked

1932 *Poetry*

"In America every**body** must have a degree," **the French man
says,** "**but t**he French do not think that all can have it; they don't
    say everyone must go to college." We
        may feel as he says we do; five kinds of superiority

might be unattainable by all, but one degree is not too much.
In each school **there is a pair of fruit-trees like that twin** tree
    in every other school: tree-of-knowledge—
        tree-of-life—each with a label like that of the other college:

lux, or *lux et veritas, Christo et ecclesiae, sapiet
felici,* **and if science confers immortality,**
    these apple-trees should be for everyone.
        Oriental arobor vitae we say lightly. Yet you pardon

it as when one thinking of the navy does not know not to infer
dishonorable discharge from a D.D. It is a
    thoughtful pupil has two thoughts for the word
        valet; or for bachelor, child, damsel; though no one having heard

**them used as terms of chivalry would make the mediaeval use of
them.** Secluded from domestic strife, Jack Bookworm led a
    college life says Goldsmith. **He might not say**
        it of the student who shows interest in the stranger's resumé

by asking "**w**hen will your experiment be finished, **Doctor Einstein**?"
and is pleased when Doctor Einstein smiles and says politely
    "science is never finished." **But we're not**
        hypocrites, we're rustics. The football huddle in the vacant lot

**is impersonating calculus and physics and military
books; and is gathering the data for genetics. If**
    scholarship would profit by it, sixteen
        foot men should be grown; it's for the football men to say. We must lean

1941 *What Are Years*

"In America," **began
the lecturer,** "every**one** must have a
degree. The** French do not think that
all can have it, they don't say everyone
      must go to college." We
do incline to feel
      that although it may be unnecessary

to know fifteen languages,
one degree is not too much. **With us, a**
school—**like the singing tree of which
the leaves were mouths singing in concert—is
both a** tree of knowledge
an**d of liberty,**—
      seen in the unanimity of college

mottoes, *lux et veritas,
Christo et ecclesiae, sapiet
felici.* **It may be that we
have not knowledge, just opinions, that** we
      are undergraduates,
not students**; we know**
      we have been told with smiles, by expatriates

of whom we had asked "When will
your experiment be finished?" "Science
is never finished." Secluded
from domestic strife, Jack Bookworm led a
      college life, says Goldsmith;
and here also as
      in France or Oxford, study is beset with

on their experience. There is vitality in the world of sport.
If it is not the tree of knowledge, it's the tree of life.
    When Audubon adopted us he taught
        us how to dance. It was the great crab-flounder of Montana caught

and changed from that which creeps to that which is angelic. He taught us how
to turn as the airport wind-sock turns without an error;
    like Alligator, Downpour, Dynamite,
        and Wotan, gliding round the course in a fast neat school, with the white

of the eye showing; or as sea-lions keep going round and round the
pool. But there is more to learn—the difference between cow
    and zebu; lion, tiger; barred and brown
        owls; horned owls have one ear that opens up and one that opens down.

The golden eagle is the one with feathered legs. The penguin wing is
ancient, not degenerate. Swordfish are different from
    gars, if one may speak of gars when the big
        gamehunters are using the fastidious singular—say pig,

and that they have seen camelsparrow, tigerhorse, rat, mouse, butterfly,
snake, elephant, fruit-bat, et cet'ra. No fact of science—
    theology or biology—might
        not as well be known; one does not care to hold opinions that fright

could dislocate. Education augments our natural forces and
prompts us to extend the machinery of advantage
    to those who are without it. One fitted
        to be a scholar must have the heroic mind, Emerson said.

The student **concentrates and does not like to fight**; "gives his opinion
firmly and rests on it"—in the manner of the poet;
    is reclusive, **and reserved;** and has such
        ways, not because he has no feeling but because he has so much.

Boasting provokes jibes, and in this country we've no cause to boast; we are
as a nation perhaps, undergraduates not students.
But anyone who studies will advance.
Are we to grow up or not? They are not all college boys in France.

dangers,—with bookworms, mildews,
and complaisancies. But someone in New
England has known enough to say
the student is patience personified,
    is a variety
of hero, "patient
    of neglect and of reproach,"—who can "hold by

himself." You can't beat hens to
make them lay. Wolf's wool is the best of wool,
but it cannot be sheared because
the wolf will not comply. With knowledge as
    with the wolf's surliness,
the student **studies**
    voluntarily, refusing to be less

than individual. He
"gives his opinion and **then** rests on it;"
he renders service where there is
no reward, and is **too** reclusive **for**
    some things to seem to touch
him, not because he
    has no feeling but because he has so much.

MARIANNE MOORE:
Half Deity

half worm. We all, infant and adult, have
stopped to watch the butterfly — last of the
 elves — and learned to spare the wingless worm
that hopefully ascends the tree. The fine-tailed
best tiger-butterfly
 of South America, with body veiled
7 in silk was that, bearing pigments which engrave
the lower wings with dragon's blood, weightless.
 They that have wings must not have weights. This more
peninsula-tailed one with a black
 pitchfork-scallop edge on sunburnt zebra-skin,
tired by the trip it made
with drover-like tenacity, has been
14 sleeping upright on the elm. Its yellowness,
that of the autumn poplar-leaf, by day
 has been observed. Disguised in butterfly-
bush Wedgewood-blue, Psyche follows it
 to that small tree, Micromalus, the midget
crab, to the mimosa,
 and from that, to the flowering pomegranate.
21 Baffled not by the quick-clouding serene gray
moon, but forced by the hot hot sun to pant,
 she stands on rug-soft grass; though "it is not
permitted to gaze informally
 on majesty, in such a manner as might
well happen here." The blind
 all-seeing butterfly, fearing the slight
28 finger, wanders — as though it were ignorant —
a step further and lights on Zephyr's palm,
 planting forefeet soberly; then pawing
like a horse, turns around — apostrophe —
 tipped brown antennae porcupining out as
it arranges nervous
 wings. Vexed because curiosity has
35 been pursuing it, it cannot now be calm.
Small unglazed china eyes of butterflies —
 pale tobacco brown — with the large eyes of
the Nymph on them; gray eyes that now are
 black, for she, with controlled agitated glance

        observes the insect's face,
          and all's a-quiver with significance
    as in the scene with cats' eyes on magpie's eyes
43 by Goya. The butterfly does not need
        home advice. As though Zephyr and Psyche
        were patent leather cricket singing
          loud and gnat-catching garden-toad side by side,
        it springs away, bewitched
          and dangerous, zebra half-deified,
49 trampling the air; as it tramples the flowers, feed-
    ing where it pivots. Twig-veined, irascible,
        fastidious, stubborn undisciplined
    zebra! Sometimes one is grateful to
        a stranger for looking very nice. But free
    to leave the breeze's hand
        it flies, drunken with triviality
56 or guided by visions of strength, away till
    diminishing like wreckage on the sea,
        rising and falling easily; mounting
        the swell and keeping its true course with
          what swift majesty, indifferent to
    us, it's gone. Deaf to my
        voice, or magnet-nice? as it flutters through
63 airs now slack, now fresh. It has strict ears when the
    West Wind speaks. It was he, with mirror eyes
        of strong anxiety, who had no net
    or flowering, shrewd-scented tropical
        device, or lignum vitae perch in half-shut
    hand; for ours is not a
        canely land; nor was it Oberon, but
70 this quiet young man with piano replies,
    named Zephyr, whose hand spread out was enough
        to tempt the fiery tiger-horse to stand,
        eyes staring skyward and chest arching
          bravely out — historic metamorphoser
    and saintly animal
        in India, in Egypt, anywhere.
77 His talk was as strange as my grandmother's muff.

75

FIGURE 2: "Psyche follows it/[...] to the mimosa"
"Half Deity" (1936), ll. 17–19

HALF DEITY

PRESENTATIONS:

Direction (Peoria, Ill.) 1 (January–March 1935): 74–75.
The Pangolin and Other Verse. London: The Brendin Publishing Co., 1936, 12–14.
What Are Years. New York: Macmillan, 1941: 17–19.
Because the variants between the 1935 and 1936 presentations are relatively minor, and the 1941 revisions significant, I have presented the former in a table and the latter in a facing-page comparison of the 1936 and 1941 presentations with material unique to each poem highlighted in bold.

TEXTUAL VARIANTS 1935–1936:

4. *Dir* fine-tailed | *POV* well-known
5. *Dir* best tiger-butterfly | *POV* silk tiger swallowtail
6–7. *Dir* veiled/in silk was that, | *POV* light-/ly furred was that
17. *Dir* Wedgewood | *POV* Wedgwood
19. *Dir* crab, [...] mimosa, | *POV* crab; [...] mimosa;
22. *Dir* moon, | *POV* moon
25. *Dir* majesty, | *POV* majesty
28. *Dir* wanders—[...] ignorant— | *POV* wanders, [...] ignorant,
29. *Dir* a step further | *POV* across the path
31. *Dir* around—apostrophe— | *POV* round—apostrophe-
36. *Dir* Small unglazed china eyes of butterflies— | *POV* The butterfly's round unglazed china eyes,
37. *Dir* brown— | *POV* brown,
38. *Dir* them; | *POV* them—
39. *Dir* she, | *POV* she
40. *Dir* face, | *POV* face
41. *Dir* significance | *POV* significance—
42–3. *Dir* as in the scene with cats' eyes on magpie's eyes/by Goya. The butterfly does | *POV* enact the scene of cats' eyes on the magpie's/eyes, by Goya. Butterflies do
45. *Dir* patent leather | *POV* patent-leather
46–8. *Dir* loud [...] garden-toad side by side,/it springs away, bewitched/and dangerous | *POV* loud, [...] garden-toad, the swallow-/tail bewitched and danger-/ous, springs away
49. *Dir* air; | *POV* air
50. *Dir* Twig-veined, irascible | *POV* Twig-veined irascible
51. *Dir* fastidious, | *POV* fastidious
54. *Dir* breeze's | *POV* outspread
56. *Dir* away till | *POV* off until,
58. *Dir* easily; mounting | *POV* easily, it mounts
61–2. *Dir* it's [...] my/voice, or magnet nice? | *POV* is [...] ap-/proval—magnet-nice,
66. *Dir* flowering, | *POV* flowering

HALF DEITY

>half worm. We all, infant and adult, have
> >stopped to watch the butterfly—last of the
> >elves—and learned to spare the wingless worm
> > >that hopefully ascends the tree. **The well-known
>silk tiger** swallowtail
> >of South America, **with body light-**
ly furred was that bearing pigments which engrave
the lower wings with dragon's blood, **weightless.**
> >They that have wings must not have weights. **This more
>peninsula-tail**ed **one** with a **black**
> >pitchfork-scallop edge **on sunburnt** zebra-**skin,
>tired by the trip it made**
> >with drover-like tenacity, **has been**
sleeping upright on the elm. Its **yellowness,**
that **of the autumn poplar**-leaf, **by day**
> >has been observed. **Disguised** in **butterfly-
>bush** Wedgwood-blue, **Psyche** follow**s it**
> > >to **that small tree, Micromalus**, the midget
>crab**; to the mimosa;**
> > >and from that, to the flowering pomegranate.
**Baffled not by the quick-clouding serene gray
moon but** forced by the **hot hot** sun to pant,
> >she stands on rug-soft grass; though **'it is** not
>permitted to gaze informally
> > >on majesty in such a manner as **might
>well happen** here'. The blind
> > >all-seeing butterfly, **fearing** the slight
>finger, **wanders,** as though it were ignorant,

1941 *What Are Years*

HALF DEITY

half worm. We all, infant and adult, have
>   stopped to watch the butterfly, last of the
>   elves, and learned to spare the wingless worm
>   >   that hopefully ascends the tree. **What zebra
>   could surpass the** zebra-
>   >   **striped** swallow-tail of South America
7   **on whose half-transparent wings, crescents** engrave

the silken edges with dragon's blood, weightless?
>   They that have wings must not have weights. **The north's
>   yellower swallow-**tail with a pitch-
>   >   fork-scallop**ed edge, has tails blunter at the tip.
>   Flying** with droverlike
>   >   tenacity **and weary from its trip,**
14 **one has lighted** on the elm. Its yellowness

that **almost counterfeits a** leaf's, has **just
>   now** been observed. **A nymph approaches, dressed**
>   in Wedgwood blue, **tries to touch it and
>   >   must** follow to *micromalus*, the midget
>   crab-**tree, to a pear-tree,**
>   >   and from that, to the flowering pomegranate.
21 **Defeated but encouraged by each new gust**

of wind, forced by the **summer** sun to pant,
>   she stands on rug-soft grass; though **some are** not
>   permitted to gaze informally
>   >   on majesty in such a manner as **she
>   is gazing** here. The blind
>   >   all-seeing butterfly, **afraid of** the
28 slight finger, **floats** as though it were ignorant,

across the path and **lights on Zephyr's** palm,
  planting forefeet soberly; then pawing
    like a horse, turns round—apostrophe-
      tipped brown antennæ porcupining out as
    it arranges nervous
      wings. **Vexed because** curiosity has
35 been pursuing it, it cannot now be calm.
  The butterfly's **round** unglazed china eyes,
    pale tobacco brown, **with the** large eyes **of**
      the Nymph **on them**—gray eyes that now are
        black, for she with controlled agitated glance
      observes the insect's face
        and all's a-quiver with significance—
42 **enact the** scene of **cats' eyes on** the magpie's
  eyes, by Goya. Butterflies do not need
    home advice. As though **Zephyr and Psyche**
      were patent-leather cricket singing
        loud, **and** gnat-catching garden-toad, the swallow-
      tail bewitched and **danger-**
        ous, springs away, **zebra half-deified,**
49 trampling the air as it tramples the flowers, feed-
  ing where it pivots. **Twig-veined** irascible
    fastidious stubborn undisciplined
      zebra! Sometimes one is grateful to
        a stranger for looking very nice. But **free**
      to leave the outspread hand
        it flies, drunken with triviality
56 or guided by visions of strength, off until,
  diminishing like wreckage on the sea,
    rising and falling easily, it mounts
      the swell and keeping its true course with
        what swift majesty, indifferent to
      us, is gone. Deaf to ap-
        proval—magnet-nice, as it flutter**s** through
63 airs now slack, now fresh. **It** has strict ears when the

across the path, and **choosing a flower's** palm
    of air and stamens, settles; then pawing
    like a horse, turns round,—apostrophe-
            tipped brown antennae porcupining out as
    it arranges nervous
            wings. **Aware that** curiosity has
35 been pursuing it, it cannot now be calm.

The butterfly's tobacco-brown unglazed
    china eyes **and furry countenance confront**
    the **n**ymph's large eyes—gray eyes that now are
            black, for she with controlled agitated glance
    explores the insect's face
            and all's a-quiver with significance.
42 **It is** Goya's scene of the **tame** magpie **faced**

by crouching cats. Butterflies do not need
    home advice. As though **the admiring nymph**
    were patent-leather cricket singing
            loud **or** gnat-catching garden-toad, the swallow-
    tail bewitched and **haughty**,
            springs away; **flies where she cannot follow,**
49 trampling the air as it trample**d** the flowers, feed-

ing where it pivots. **Equine** irascible
    unwormlike unteachable butterfly-
    zebra! Sometimes one is grateful to
            a stranger for looking very nice; **to** the
    friendly outspread hand. But
            it flies, drunken with triviality
56 or guided by visions of strength, off until,

diminishing like wreckage on the sea,
    rising and falling easily, it mounts
    the swell and keeping its true course with
            what swift majesty, indifferent to
    her, is gone. Deaf to ap-
            proval, magnet-nice as it fluttere**d** through
63 airs now slack now fresh, **it** ha**d** strict ears when the

1936

West Wind **speaks. It was he, with mirror eyes**
    of strong anxiety, who had no net
    or flowering shrewd-scented tropical
        device, or lignum vitæ perch in half-shut
    hand; for ours is not a
        canely land; nor was **it** Oberon, but
70   this quiet **young man** with piano replies,
    named Zephyr, whose **hand spread out** was enough
        to tempt the fiery tiger-horse to stand,
        eyes staring skyward and chest arching
            bravely out—historic metamorphoser
    and saintly animal
        in India, in Egypt, anywhere.
77   **His** talk was as strange as my grandmother's muff.

1941

west wind **spoke; for pleased by the butterfly's**
    inconsequential ease, he held no net,
    did not regard the butterfly-bush
        as a trap, hid no decoy in half-shut
    palm since his is not a
        covetous hand. It was **not** Oberon, but
70 this quiet**est wind** with piano replies,

the zephyr, whose **detachment** was enough
    to tempt the fiery tiger-horse to stand,
    eyes staring skyward and chest arching
        bravely out—historic metamorphoser
    and saintly animal
        in India, in Egypt, anywhere.
77 **Their** talk was as strange as my grandmother's muff.

Smooth Gnarled Crepe Myrtle!

BY MARIANNE MOORE

A brass-green bird with grass-
green throat smooth as a nut, springs from
   twig to twig askew, copying the
   Chinese flower piece—businesslike atom
   in the stiff-leafed tree's blue-
pink, dregs-of-wine, pyramids
   of mathematic
      circularity—one of a
   pair. A redbird with a hatchet
   crest lights straight, on a twig
   between the two, bending the
      peculiar
         bouquet down; and there are

several black antique
bootjack fireflies touched with weak bright
   hunting-pink. " The legendary white-
eared black bulbul that sings
   only in pure Sanskrit " should
be here—" tame clever
   true nightingale." The cardinal-
   bird that is usually a
   pair looks somewhat odd, like
" the ambassadorial
   Inverness
worn by one who dresses

in New York but dreams of
London." It was artifice saw
   on the china thimble-box, room for
fervent script, and wrote as with a bird's claw
   under the pair on the
hyacinth-blue lid—" joined in
   friendship, crowned by love."
   An aspect may deceive; as the
   elephant's columbine-tubed trunk
   held waveringly out—
      an at will heavy thing—is
         delicate.
   Art is unfortunate.

One may be a blameless
bachelor and it is but a
   step to Congreve. A Rosalindless
redbird comes where people are, knowing they
   have not made a point of
   being where he is—this bird
   which says not sings, " without loneliness I should be more
   lonely, so I keep it "—half in
   Japanese. And what of
   our clasped hands that swear " By Peace
      Plenty; as
         by Wisdom Peace." Alas.

The poem entitled " Trophy for a Tyrant," published
in our issue of last week, is by C. A. Millspaugh.

Speech Rhythms and Idiom

By D. G. BRIDSON

Poetic drama as a contemporary possibility dates from metric's first taking up with the rhythms and idiom of contemporary speech. Whether or not the elastic common-stock of blank verse is capable of those rhythms and that idiom is a question largely dependent upon one's own particular ideas upon blank verse. Mr. MacLeish, whose new play, " Panic," represents one more poet's attempt to put Broadway on Broadway, opines that it is not : " The reason is, that the rhythm of blank verse and the rhythms of the spoken language of our (his) country are precisely opposed. The rhythm of blank verse is spacious, slow, noble and elevated. It moves forward in muscular iambic march. Even when interrupted, even when passionate, blank verse is always marmoreal—an hysteria of statues. It is the poetic counterpart of a language—but of a language spoken in deliberate ages by violent and deliberate men : men ceremonial even in their hatreds, deliberate even in their laughter. The rhythms of contemporary American speech on the other hand are nervous, not muscular; excited, not deliberate; vivid, not proud. To my ear—and a man can only testify after his own senses—the classical rhythm equivalent to American speech would be more nearly the trochee or the dactyl than the iamb of blank verse."

" Panic," then, represents—technically—an attempt to catch the rhythms of contemporary speech in trochaic or dactylic metric. I say trochaic or dactylic for the good reason that Mr. MacLeish, rightly ignoring syllabic quantity in more logical reliance on accentual, rates them as mere name-variants of the same essential thing. (In this, by the way, he happens to follow a theory at least as old—even in " modern " verse—as Coleridge's " Christabel.") For the character parts he uses a line of five beats or accents, in which the number of syllables may vary from five to an odd seventeen. For the antiphonal choruses, he uses a line of three beats. To quote him finally, "the voices of men talking intently to each other in the offices or the mills or on the streets of this country *descend from* stressed syllables; they do not *rise toward* stressed syllables as do the voices of men speaking in Shakespeare's plays."

Whatever we say of this last theory (I personally disagree with it) one is bound to admit that Mr. MacLeish's experiment is extremely interesting. That he has caught hold of the rhythms of normal speech is matter of certain fact. But whether those rhythms are trochaic-dactylic or iambic-anapaestic, remains matter of some doubt. The following, from a typical antiphon, doesn't seem to get us very far :

> Nevertheless it's an
> Ill name to be light with!
> Which of us knows the why or the
> When or the where either of
> What's moving beneath in the
> Trouble of times? It might be
> Men in the past were right and
> Fate does drive us! Covered with

SMOOTH GNARLED CREPE MYRTLE!

PRESENTATIONS:

New English Weekly, 8 (17 October 1935): 13.
Smoke, 5 (Winter 1936): 5–6.
The Pangolin and Other Verse. London: The Brendin Publishing Co., 1936, 15–16.
What Are Years. New York: Macmillan, 1941: 20–21.

TEXTUAL VARIANTS 1935–1941:

ti. *NewE* "Smooth Gnarled Crepe Myrtle!" | *Sm, POV , WAY* "Smooth Gnarled Crape Myrtle" | *POV* "Smooth Gnarled Crape Myrtle" Grouped fourth, with "Virginia Britannia," "Bird-Witted," and "Half Deity" under the title "The Old Dominion."

4. *NewE, Sm, POV* piece— | *WAY* piece,—
6. *NewE, Sm, POV* pink, [...] wine, | *WAY* pink [...] wine
8. *NewE, Sm, POV* circularity— | *WAY* circularity;
14–6. *NewE, Sm, POV* several black antique/bootjack fireflies touched with weak bright/hunting-pink. | *WAY* moths and lady-bugs and/a boot-jack firefly with black wings/and pink head.
22. *NewE, Sm, POV* pair | *WAY* pair,
27. *NewE, Sm, POV* saw | *WAY* saw,
28. *NewE* the china thimble-box | *Sm* a patch-box-pigeon-egg | *POV, WAY* a patch-box pigeon-egg
31. *NewE, WAY* "joined *Sm* "joined | *POV* 'joined
40. *NewE, Sm, POV* bachelor | *WAY* bachelor,
41. *NewE, POV, WAY* step | *Sm* stop
45. *NewE, WAY* "with *Sm* with | *POV* 'with
49. *NewE, Sm, POV* swear | *WAY* swear,
51. *NewE, Sm* Alas. | *POV, WAY* Alas!

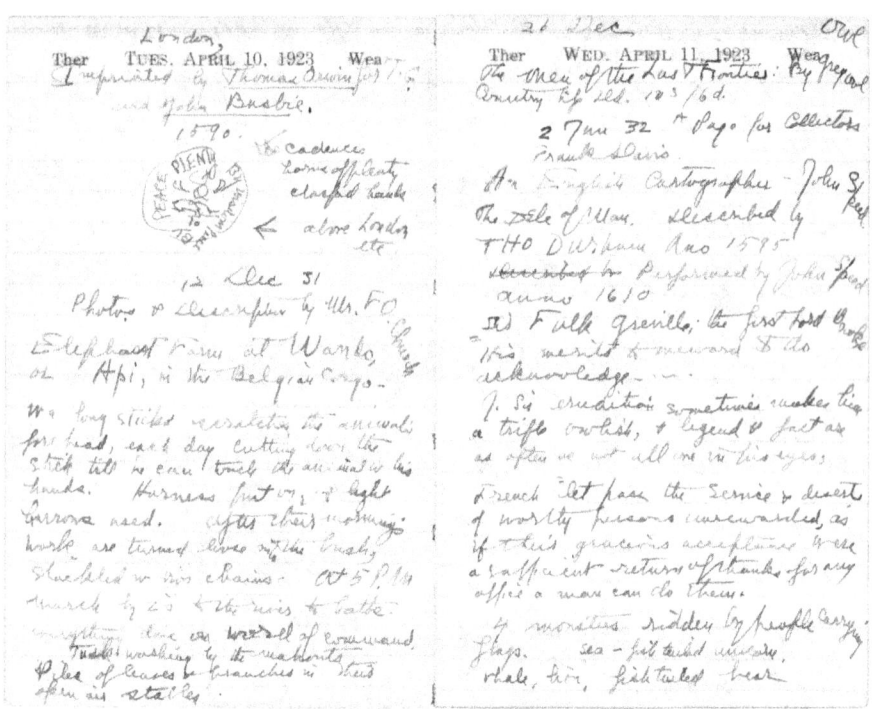

FIGURES 3 AND 4: "And what of/our clasped hands that swear
'By Peace/Plenty; as/by Wisdom Peace.'"
"Smooth Gnarled Crepe Myrtle!" (1935): ll. 48–51

Adversity and Grace

POETRY

Virginia Britannia

PALE sand edges England's old
   dominion. The air is soft, warm, hot,
     above the cedar-dotted emerald shore
known to the redbird,
   the redcoated musketeer,
     the trumpet-flower, the cavalier,
the parson, and the
     wild parishioner. A deer-
track in a church-floor
brick and Sir George Yeardley's
coffin-tacks and
tomb remain. The now tremendous vine-
encompassed hackberry
     starred with the ivy-flower,
     shades the church tower.
And " a great sinner lyeth here " under the sycamore.

A silver-bordered fritil-
lary zigzags toward the resting-place
   of this unusual and pleasing man, who
" waits for a joyful
     resurrection." We-re-wo-
     comoco's fur crown could be no
odder than we were
     with ostrich, Latin motto,
   and small gold horse-shoe,
as arms for an able
sting-ray-hampered
   pioneer (painted as a Turk it
seems) the incessantly
     exciting Captain Smith
     who patient with
his inferiors, was a pugna-
     cious equal ; and to

Powhatan, obliged but not
a flatterer. (Rare Indian, crowned by
   Christopher Newport !) The Old Dominion has
all-green grass-hoppers

40   in all-green, box-sculptured grounds ;
      an almost English green surrounds
      them. Care has formed, a-
         mong unEnglish insect sounds,
      the white wall-rose. As
      thick as Daniel Boone's grape-
      vine, the stem has
46   wide-spaced great blunt alternating os-
      trich-skin warts that were thorns.
            Care has formed walls of yew
            since Indians knew
      the Fort Old Field and narrow neck of
51   land that Jamestown was.

      Observe the terse Virginian,
      the mettlesome gray one that drives the
         owl from tree to tree and imitates the call
      of whippoorwill or
         lark or katydid—the lead-
57   gray lead-legged mocking-bird with head
      held half away, and
         meditative eye as dead
         as sculptured marble
      eyes. Alighting noiseless-
      ly it muses
63   in the semi sun, on tall thin legs,
      as if it did not see,
            still standing there alone
            on the round stone-
      topped table with lead cupids grouped to
68   form the pedestal.

      Narrow herring-bonelaid bricks,
      a dusty pink beside the dwarfbox-
         bordered pansies, share the ivy-arbor shade
      with cemetery
         lace settees, one at each side,
74   and with the bird : box-bordered tide-
      water gigantic
         jet black pansies (splendor ; pride ;)
         not for a decade
      dressed, but for a day—in
      overpowering
80   velvet ; and gray Blue-Andalusi
      an-cock-feather pale ones
            ink-lined on the edge, fur-

eyed, with ochre
on the cheek.   The slowmoving glossy
85   saddle-cavalcade

of buckeye-brown surprising
jumpers ; the contrasting work-mule and
  show-mule and witch-cross door and " **strong sweet prison,**"
are a part of what
  has come about, in the Black
91   idiom, from advancing back-
ward in a circle ;
  from taking The Potomac
  cowbirdlike ; and on
The Chickahominy
establishing
97   the Negro (opportunely brought) to
strengthen protest against
      tyranny. Rare unscent-
      ed, provident-
ly hot, too sweet, inconsistent flower-
102   bed ! Old Dominion

earth makes sunflower-heads grow large ;
hibiscus and so-called mimosa
  close at night ; the scarlet peculiarly-quilled
pomegranate-petals,
      the African violet,
108   and camellia, perfumeless. Yet
house-high glistening green
      magnolia-trees with velvet-
      textured flower, are filled
with anaesthetic scent
enough to make
114   one die ; as the gardenia is though
its two-toned green-furled buds,
      and dark leaf-vein on green-
      er leaf when seen
against the light, attract no pigmy
119   bees such as the frilled

silk substanceless faint flower of
the crepe-myrtle does. Queen of the Pa-
  munkeys, birdclaw-earringd ; with a pet raccoon
from The Mattapo-
      ni (what a bear) ! Feminine,
125   odd, Indian young lady ! Odd thin-

gauge-and-taffeta-
   dressed English one! Terrapin
 meat and crested spoon
feed the mistress of French
plum-and-turquoise-
131   piped chaise-longue; of brass-knobbed slat front door
and everywhere open
   shaded house on Indian-
      named Virginian
streams, in counties named for English lords!
136   The rattlesnake soon

said from our once dashingly
undiffident first flag, " don't tread on
   me," tactless symbol of a new republic.
Priorities were
   cradled in this region not
      noted for humility; spot
142 that has high-singing
   frogs, cotton-mouth snakes and cot-
ton-fields; clay for brick,
Lawrence jugs with Persian
loping wolf de-
148 sign; and hounds. Here the poor unpoison-
ous terrapin likes to
   idle near the sea-top;
      tobacco-crop
gains have church tablets; Devil's woodyard
153   swamps and one-brick-thick-

wall serpentine shadows star-
tle strangers.   Strangler fig, pale fiercely
   unpretentious North American, and Dutch
trader, and noble
   Roman, in taking what they
159   pleased—colonizing as we say—
were not all intel-
   lect and delicacy. A
black savage or such
as was subject to the
deer-fur Crown is
165 not all brawn and animality.
The limestone tea-table,
   the mandolin-shaped big
      and little fig,
and the now disused silkworm-trees, show
170   intelligence; much

104   *Adversity and Grace*

kind tyranny made ha-ha-s
that kept back cows ; clock-strengthened stocking
   and drooping cotton dress with handmade edge mark
tyrant taste. The song-
     bird wakes too soon, to enjoy
       excellent idleness, destroy-
ing legitimate
     laziness, the unbought toy
  even in the dark
risking loud whee whee whee
of joy, the car-
away-seed-spotted sparrow perched in
the dew-drenched juniper
      beside the window-ledge ;
      the little hedge-
sparrow that wakes up seven minutes
   sooner than the lark

they say. The live-oak's moss-draped
undulating massiveness, the white
   pine, the English hackberry—handsomest vis-
itor of all, the
     cedar's etched solidity,
     the cypress, lose identity
and are one tree, as
     sunset flames increasingly
  over the leaf-chis-
selled blackening ridge of green.
Expanding to
earth size, igniting redundantly
wind-widened clouds, it can
      not move bothered-with-wages
    new savages,
but gives the child an intimation
   of what glory is.

                                    MARIANNE MOORE

FIGURE 5: "The scarlet much-quilled/fruiting pomegranate"
"Virginia Britannia" (1941), ll. 105–6

VIRGINIA BRITANNIA

PRESENTATIONS:

Life and Letters Today, 13 (December 1935): 66–70.
The Pangolin and Other Verse. London: The Brendin Publishing Co., 1936, 3–9.
What Are Years. New York: Macmillan, 1941: 25–32.

TEXTUAL VARIANTS 1935–1941:

The syllable distribution changes between presentations in the last seven lines of each stanza. The line breaks are re-arranged to accommodate the syllable redistributions. With minor variations, the syllable patterns for the affected lines are as follows: *Li*: 4–9–6–7–5–9–5 | *POV, WAY*: 7–7–5–7–5–10–4. There is one further significant variant, in stanza 6: 96–102. *Li* 4–9–6–6–4–10–5 | 96–101. *POV* 14–5–6–4–11–4 | 96–102. *WAY* 7–7–5–6–4–11–4.

Where the revisions to this poem are too extensive to be enumerated by line, as in the last four stanzas of the 1941 presentation, I have provided side-by-side comparisons, with material that differs from or is unique to the *What Are Years* presentation marked in bold.

1–2.	*Li, POV* old/dominion	*WAY* Old/Dominion
5.	*Li, POV* redcoated	*WAY* red-coated
10–12.	*Li* brick and Sir George Yeardley's/coffin-tacks and/tomb	10–11. *POV* brick and Sir George Yeardley's/coffin-tacks and tomb	10–11. *WAY* brick, and a fine pavement-/tomb with engraved top,
18–20.	*Li* silver-bordered fritil-/lary zigzags toward the resting-place/of this unusual and pleasing man,	*POV* fritillary zigzags/toward the seemly resting-place of this/unusual man and pleasing sinner	*WAY* fritillary zigzags/toward the chancel-shaded resting-place/of this unusual man and sinner
22.	*Li, POV* We-re-wo-	*WAY* We-rewo-
24.	*Li, POV* were	*WAY* were,
29–30.	*Li* pioneer (painted […] "Turk it" seems)	28–9. *POV* pioneer,/painted […] "Turk it" seems,	28–29. *WAY* pioneer—/painted […] "Turk, it" seems—
30.	*Li, POV* the incessantly	*WAY* continuously
32.	*Li, POV* who	*WAY* who,
34.	Li, POV equal;	WAY equal,
35–6.	*Li* Powhatan, obliged but not/a flatterer. *POV* Powhatan obliged, but not/a flatterer.	*WAY* Powhatan as unflatter-/ing as grateful.
36–7.	*Li* (Rare […] Newport!)	*POV , WAY* Rare […] Newport!
38.	*Li, POV* grass-hoppers	*WAY* grasshoppers
39–40.	*Li, POV* all-green, […] grounds;/an	*WAY* all-green […] grounds./An
41.	*Li* formed,	*POV , WAY* formed

61–5.	*Li* eyes. Alighting noiseless-/ly it muses/in the semi sun, on tall thin legs,/ as if it did not see,/still standing there alone	*POV* eye, alighting noiseless,/ muses in the semi-sun,/standing on tall thin legs as/if he did not see,/ conspicuous, alone,	*WAY* eye, alighting noiseless,/musing in the semi-sun,/standing on tall thin legs as/if he did not see,/conspicuous, alone,
69.	*Li, POV* herring-bonelaid	*WAY* herring-bone-laid
70.	*Li* dwarfbox	*POV, WAY* dwarf box
76.	*Li* (splendor; pride;)	*POV* (splendour; pride;)	*WAY* —splendor; pride—
78.	*Li* day—	*POV* , *WAY* day,
80–1.	*Li* gray Blue-Andalusi/an-cock-feather	*POV* gray blue-Andalusian/cock-feather	*WAY* gray-blue-Andalusian-/cock-feather
84–5.	*Li* slowmoving glossy/saddle-cavalcade *POV* slowmoving glossy, tall/quick cavalcade	*WAY* at first slow, saddle-horse/quick cavalcade
86.	*Li, POV* buckeye-brown surprising	*WAY* buckeye-burnished
87.	*Li* jumpers; the contrasting	*POV* jumpers, the contrasting	*WAY* 86–7. jumpers/and five-gaited mounts, the
88.	*Li* and […] and […] "strong […] prison,"	*POV* & […] & […] 'strong […] prison'	*WAY* and […] and […] 'strong […] prison'
89.	*Li , WAY* are a part	*POV* are part
90–1.	*Li, POV* about, in […] idiom,	*WAY* about—in […] idiom—
91–2.	*Li, POV* advancing back-/ward […] circle;	*WAY* "advancin' back-/wards […] circle;"
94.	*Li, POV* cowbirdlike;	*WAY* cowbirdlike,
97–8.	*Li* Negro (opportunely brought) to/strengthen protest against	96–7. *POV* Negro, opportunely brought, to strength-/en protest against	*WAY* 96–8. Negro,/inadvertent ally and/best enemy of
101–2.	*Li* flower-/bed!	100. *POV* flowerbed!	101. *WAY* flower-bed!
103–12.	*Li*, 102–11. *POV* **earth makes sunflower-heads grow large;** **hibiscus and so-called mimosa**

    close at night; the scarlet **peculiarly**-quilled
pomegranate-**petals**,
    the African violet,
    and camellia, perfume**less**. Yet
house-high glistening green
    magnolia-**trees with** velvet-
    textured flower, **are** filled
with anaesthetic scent

103–12.	*WAY* **flowers are curious. Some wilt** **in daytime and some close at night. Some**

    have perfume; **some have not.** The scarlet **much**-quilled
fruiting pomegranate,
    the African violet,
    fuschia and camellia, **none;** yet
the house-high glistening
    green magnolia**'s** velvet-
    textured flower **is** filled
with anaesthetic scent

113–9. *Li* **enough to make
one die;** as the gardenia **is though
its two-toned green-furled buds,**
    and dark leaf-vein on green-
    er leaf when seen
against the light, **attract no pigmy
bees such as** |

112–8. *POV* **enough to make one die;** as
the gardenia **is, though its
two-toned green-furled buds**
    and dark leaf-vein on green-
    er leaf when seen
against the light **attract no pigmy** bees
such as |

113–9. *WAY* **as inconsiderate** as
the gardenia**'s. Even the
gardenia, a-**
    gainst dark leaf-vein on green-
    er leaf when seen
against the light, **has not near it more small
bees, than**

121–2. *Li* crepe-myrtle does. Queen of the Pa-/munkeys, birdclaw-earringd | 120–1. *POV* crape-myrtle does. Odd Pamunkey/princess, birdclaw-earringed | 121–2 *WAY* crape-myrtle has. Odd Pamunkey/princess, birdclaw-earringed

123. *Li*, 122. *POV* The | 123. *WAY* the
124. *Li* bear)! Feminine, | 123. *POV* , 124. *WAY* bear!) Feminine
125. *Li* odd, | 124. *POV*, 125. *WAY* odd
131. *Li* front door | 130. *POV*, 131. *WAY* front-door
135. *Li* streams, [...] lords! | 134. *POV* streams, [...] lords. | 134. *WAY* streams [...] lords.
139. *Li*, 138. *POV* me," | 139. *WAY* me,"—
145. *Li*, 144. *POV* clay for brick, | 145. *WAY* a unique
146. *Li*, 145. *POV* jugs with Persian | 146. *WAY* pottery with

TEXTUAL VARIANTS 1935–1936

These variants represent changes between the *Life and Letters Today* and *The Pangolin and Other Verse* presentations.

155–7. *Li* Strangler fig, pale fiercely/unpretentious North American, and Dutch/trader, and | 154–6. *POV* The strangler fig, the dwarf-/fancying Egyptian, the American,/the Dutch, the
169–70. *Li* show/intelligence | 168–9. *POV* imply/amity
171. *Li* ha-ha-s | 170. *POV* ha-has
173. *Li* edge | 172. *POV* edge,
174. *Li* taste. The | 173. *POV* taste; the
178. *Li* the unbought | 177. *POV* this unbought

188–204. *Li* they say. The live-oak's **moss-draped**
undulating **massiveness**, the white
    pine, the **English** hackberry—handsomest vis-
itor of all**,** the
    cedar's etched solidity,
    the cypress, lose identity
and are one tree, as
    sunset flames increasingly
over the leaf-chis-
selled blackening ridge of green**.**
Expanding to
earth size**, igniting** redundantly
wind-widened clouds**, it can**
    not move bothered-with-wages
    new savages,
but gives the child an intimation
of what glory is.

187–203. *POV* they say. The live oak's **rounded**
mass of undulating **boughs,** the white
    pine, the **agèd** hackberry—handsomest vis-
itor of all—the
    cedar's etched solidity,
    the cypress, lose identity
and are one tree, as
    sunset flames increasingly
against their leaf-chis-
elled blackening ridge of green;
and the redundantly wind-
widened clouds **e**xpanding to
earth size **above the**
    town's bothered with wages
    childish sages,
are to the child an intimation of
what glory is.

VARIANTS 1941

These variants represent material that is unique to the *What Are Years* presentation, as compared to that in *The Pangolin and Other Verse*.

147–204. design; and **too**
unvenomous terrapin
in tepid greenness,
    idl**ing** near the sea-top;
    tobacco-crop
records on church **walls; a** Devil's Woodyard**;**
and **the** one-brick-

thick serpentine wall **built by**
Jefferson. Like **s**trangler fig**s choking**
    a banyan, not an explorer, no impe-
rialist, not one
    of us, in taking what **we**
    pleased—**in** colonizing as **the**
saying is—**has been**
    a synonym for mercy.
   The redskin with the deer-
fur **c**rown**, famous for his**
cruelty, is not all brawn
and animality. The
outdoor tea-table,
    the mandolin-shaped big
    and little fig,
the silkworm-**mulberry, the French mull dress**
    with the Madei-

ra-vine **accompanied** edge**, are**
when compared with what the colonists
    found here in Tidewater Virginia, stark
luxuries. The mere
    brown hedge-sparrow, with reckless
    ardor, unable to suppress
his satisfaction
    in man's trustworthy nearness,
   even in the dark
flutes his ecstatic burst
of joy—the caraway-seed-
spotted sparrow perched in the
dew-drenched juniper
    beside the window-ledge;
    this little hedge-
sparrow that wakes up seven minutes sooner than the lark**.**

The live oak's **darkening fila-
gree** of undulating boughs, the etched
    solidity **of a** cypress **indivis-
ible from** the **now**
        agèd **English** hackberry,
    become with lost identity,
part of the ground, as
        sunset flames increasingly
    against the leaf-chis-
selled blackening ridge of green;
while clouds, expanding above
the town's **assertiveness, dwarf
it, dwarf arrogance**
        **that can misunderstand
        importance; and**
are to the child an intimation of
what glory is.

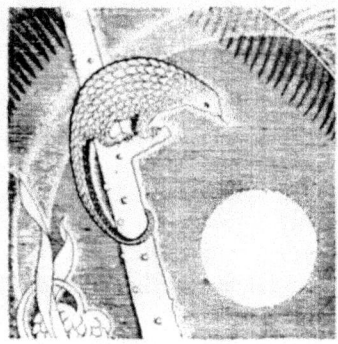

THE PANGOLIN

Another armoured animal—scale
    lapping scale with spruce-cone regu-
    larity until they
form the uninterrupted central
    tail-row. This near artichoke
    with head and legs and grit-equipped giz-
zard, the night miniature artist-
    engineer, is   Leonardo's
    indubitable son? Im-
pressive animal
and toiler, of whom we seldom hear.
    Armour seems extra. But for him,
the closing ear-
    ridge—or bare
    ear, lacking even this small
    eminence—and similarly safe

contracting nose and eye apertures
    impenetrably closable,
    are not;—a true ant-eat-
er, not cockroach-eater, who endures
    exhausting solitary
        trips through unfamiliar ground at night,

(17)

The Pangolin and Other Verse. London: The Brendin Publishing Co., 1936: 17–21.

                    returning before sunrise; stepping
24   in the moonlight,   on the moonlight
                        peculiarly, that the out-
                    side edges of his
                    hands may bear the weight and save the claws
                            for digging. Serpentined about
                    the tree, he draws
                        away from
                        danger unpugnaciously,
32   with no sound but a harmless hiss; keep-

                    ing the fragile grace of the Thomas-
                            of-Leighton-Buzzard Westminster
                            Abbey wrought-iron vine, or
                    rolls himself into a ball that has
                        power to defy all effort
                            to unroll it;—strongly intailed, neat
                            head for core, on neck not breaking off,
40   with curled-in feet.   Nevertheless
                            he has sting-proof scales; and nest
                        of rocks closed with earth
                    from inside, which he can thus darken.
                            Sun and moon & day and night &
                            man and beast
                    each with a splen-
                        dour which man
                        in all his vileness cannot
48   set aside; each with an excellence!

                    'Fearful yet to be feared,' the armoured
                        ant-eater met by the driver
                        ant does not turn back, but
                    engulfs what he can, the flattened sword-
                        edged leafpoints on the tail and
                            artichoke-set leg and body plates
                        quivering violently when it
56   retaliates   and swarms on him.

(18)

             Compact like the furled fringed frill
          on the hat-brim of
    Gargallo's hollow iron head of a
             matador, he will drop and will
       then walk away
          unhurt, al-
          though if unintruded on
          he will come slowly down the tree, helped

    by his tail. The giant-pangolin
          tail, graceful tool, as prop or hand
          or broom or axe, tipped like
    the elephant's trunk with special skin,
          is not lost on this ant and
             stone swallowing uninjurable
          artichoke, which simpletons thought a
             living fable   whom the stones had
                nourished whereas ants had done
          so. Pangolins are
    not aggressive animals; between
             dusk and day, they have the not un-
       chainlike, machine-
          like form and
          frictionless creep of a thing
          made graceful by adversities, con-

    versities. To explain grace requires
          a curious hand. If that which
          is at all were not for
    ever, why would those who graced the spires
          with animals and gathered
             there to rest, on cold luxurious
          low stone steats—a monk and monk and monk—
             between the thus   ingenious roof-
                supports, have slaved to confuse
          grace with a kindly
    manner, time in which to pay a debt,
          the cure for sins, a graceful use

                      (19)

                    of what are yet
                    approved stone
                    mullions branching out across
                        the perpendiculars? A sailboat
                was the first machine. The manis, made
                    for moving quietly also,
                    is neither a prisoner
                nor a god; on hind feet plantigrade,
                    with certain postures of a
                        man. Beneath sun and moon, man slaving
                    to make his life more sweet, leaves half the
                        flowers worth having,   needing to choose
                        wisely how to use the strength;—
                a paper-maker
                like the wasp; a tractor of food-stuffs,
                        like the ant; spidering a length
                of web from bluffs
                    above a
                    stream; in fighting, mechanicked
                    like the pangolin; capsizing in

            disheartenment. Bedizened or stark
                naked, man, the self, the being
                so-called human, writing-
            master to this world, griffons a dark
                    'Like does not like like that is
                    obnoxious'; and writes errror with four
                r's. Among animals, one has a
                    sense of humour   then, which saves a
                    few steps, which saves years—unig-
                norant, modest and
            unemotional, and all emo-
                    tion; one with everlasting vig-
                our, power to grow
                    though there are
                    few of him—who can make one
                    breathe faster, and make one erecter.

                            (20)

Not afraid of anything is he
    and then goes cowering forth, tread paced
    to meet an obstacle
at every step. Consistent with the
    formula—warm blood, no gills,
        two pairs of hands and a few hairs—that
    is a mammal; there he sits in his
        own habitat,   serge-clad, strong-shod.
            The prey of fear; he, always
    curtailed, extinguished,
thwarted by the dusk, work partly done,
    says to the alternating blaze,
'Again the sun!
    anew each
    day; and new and new and new,
        that comes into and steadies my soul.'

(21)

THE PANGOLIN

PRESENTATIONS:

The Pangolin and Other Verse. London: The Brendin Publishing Co., 1936: 17–21.
Living Age 360 (July 1941): 500.
What Are Years. New York: Macmillan, 1941: 39–43.

TEXTUAL VARIANTS 1936–1941:

The sixth, ninth, and twelfth lines of each stanza are justified differently in the *Living Age* presentation.

ti.   *POV, WAY* "The Pangolin" | *Liv Living Age* reprints only the final stanza of the poem, under the title "The Being So-Called Human."

9.   *POV* son? | *WAY* son.
15. *POV* ear | *WAY* ear
44. *POV* moon & day [...] night& man | *WAY* moon and day [...] night and man
64. *POV* will come slowly | *WAY* cautiously works
64. *POV* pangolin | *WAY* pangolin-
70. *POV* stone swallowing | *WAY* stone-swallowing
71. *POV* artichoke, | *WAY* artichoke
73. *POV* nourished | *WAY* nourished,
77. *POV* chainlike, | *WAY* chainlike
96–7. *POV* no space between lines 96 and 97 *WAY* space between lines 96 and 97 to indicate stanza break
97. *POV* The manis | *WAY* Pangolins
99–100. *POV* is neither a prisoner/nor a god; on [...] plantigrade, | *WAY* are models of exactness,/on four legs; or [...] plantigrade
115. *POV* so-called | *WAY* we call
120. *POV* humour then, which | *WAY* humor. Humor
121. *POV* which [...] years—unig- | *WAY* it [...] years. Unig-
124. *POV* tion; one with | *WAY* tion, he has
127. *POV* of him— | *WAY* creatures
136. *POV, WAY* caesura after fourth syllable *Liv* no caesura
137. *POV, Liv* fear; | *WAY* fear,
138. *POV, WAY* extinguished, | *Liv* extinguished

Adversity and Grace

SEE IN THE MIDST OF FAIR LEAVES

Marianne Moore

and much fruit, the swan—
    one line of the mathematician's
sign greater-than, drawn
    to an apex where the lake is
met by the weight on it; or an angel
standing in the sun, how well
7   armed, how manly;

and promenading
    in sloughs of despond, a monster—
man when human nothing
    more, grown to immaturity,
punishing debtors, seeking his due—as
an arrow turned inward has
14   no chance of peace.

New Directions in Prose and Poetry. Ed. James Laughlin. Norfolk, Conn.: New Directions, 1936, [56].

SEE IN THE MIDST OF FAIR LEAVES

PRESENTATIONS:

New Directions in Prose and Poetry. Ed. James Laughlin. Norfolk, Conn.: New Directions, 1936, [56].
What Are Years. New York: Macmillan, 1941: 33.

TEXTUAL VARIANTS 1936–1941:

3. *ND* greater-than, | *WAY* greater-than
6. *ND* sun, | *WAY* sun;
9. *ND* monster— | *WAY* monster,
12. *ND* due— | *WAY* due

Bird-Witted

With innocent wide penguin eyes, three
    grown fledgling mocking-birds below
the pussy-willow tree,
    stand in a row,
wings touching, feebly solemn,
till they see
        their no longer larger
        mother bringing
something which will partially
feed one of them.
Towards the high-keyed intermittent squeak
    of broken carriage-springs, made by
the three similar, meek-
        coated bird's-eye
freckled forms she comes; and when
from the beak
        of one, the still living
        beetle has dropped
out, she picks it up and puts
it in again.
Standing in the shade till they have dressed
    their thickly-filamented, pale
pussy-willow-surfaced
    coats, they spread tail
and wings, showing one by one,
the modest
        white stripe lengthwise on the
        tail and crosswise
underneath the wing, and the
accordion
is closed again. What delightful note
    with rapid unexpected flute-
sounds leaping from the throat
    of the astute
grown bird comes back to one from
the remote
        unenergetic sun-
        lit air before
the brood was here? Why has the
bird's voice become
harsh? A piebald cat observing them,
    is slowly creeping toward the trim
trio on the tree-stem.
    Unused to him
the three make room—uneasy
new problem.
        A dangling foot that missed
        its grasp, is raised
and finds the twig on which it
planned to perch. The
parent darting down, nerved by what chills
    the blood, and by hope rewarded—
of toil—since nothing fills
    squeaking unfed
mouths, wages deadly combat,
and half kills
        with bayonet beak and
        cruel wings, the
intellectual cautious-
l y   c r e e p i n g   c a t.

                MARIANNE MOORE.

New Republic, 85 (22 January 1936): 311.

BIRD-WITTED

PRESENTATIONS:

New Republic, 85 (22 January 1936): 311.
The Pangolin and Other Verse. London: The Brendin Publishing Co., 1936, 10–11.
What Are Years. New York: Macmillan, 1941: 22–24.

TEXTUAL VARIANTS 1936–1941:

WAY Spacing between ten-line stanzas.| *NewR, POV* No spacing.

2. *NewR, POV* grown | *WAY* large
11. *NewR, POV* Towards | *WAY* Toward
29. *NewR, WAY* underneath the | *POV* on the under
35. *NewR, POV* bird | *POV* bird,
59. *NewR, WAY* intellectual | *POV* intellectual,

Vol. XLIX
No. II

PRIZE-AWARD NUMBER

NOVEMBER 1936

WALKING-STICKS AND PAPERWEIGHTS
AND WATERMARKS

WALKING AMONG sceptre-headed
   weeds and daisies swayed by wind, they said,
    "Don't scatter your
stick, on account of the souls." Led
from sun-spotted
   paths, we went "where leafy trees meet
   overhead and noise of traffic is unknown"—
the mind exhilarated
    by life all round, so stirringly

alive. The root-handled cudgel
with the bark left on, the woodbine smell-
   ing of the rain,
the very stones, have life. Little
¹⁴ scars on church-bell
   tongues put there by the Devil's claws —
   authentic phantoms, ghosts, and witches, transformed
into an invisible
¹⁸   fabric of inconsistency

motheaten by self-subtractives —
now as outright murderers and thieves,
   thrive openly.
An epigraph before it leaves
²³ the wax, receives
   to give, and giving must itself
   receive, "difficulty is ordained to check
poltroons," and courage achieves
²⁷   despaired of ends. Oppositely

jointed against indecision,
the three legs of the triskelion
   meeting in the
middle between triangles, run
³² in unison
   without assistance. Yet, trudging
   on two legs that move contradictorily,
irked by ghosts and witches, one
³⁶   does not fear to ask for beauty

[60]

that is power devoid of fear.
A bold outspoken gentleman, cheer-
    ful, plodding, to-
the-point, used to the atmosphere
of work — who here
    appropriate to the thought of
    permanence, says, "this is my taste, it might not
be another man's"— makes clear
    that stark sincere unflattery,

sine cera, is both farthest
from self-defensiveness and nearest;
    as when a seal
without haste, slowly is impressed
and forms a nest
    on which the raised device reversed,
    shows round. It must have been an able workman,
studious and self-possessed,
    a liker of solidity,

who gave a greenish Waterford
glass fool's cap with summit curled down toward
    itself as the
glass grew, the look of tempered sword-
steel, and three-ore-d
    fishscale-burnished antimony-
    tin-and-lead's smoky water-drop type-metal
smoothness emery-armored
    against rust. Its subdued glossy

[61]

splendor leaps out at the eye as
form dramatizes thought, in the glass
    witchball and air-
twist cane. This paperweight, in mass
68 a stone, surpass-
    ing it in tint, enlarges the
    fine chain-lines in the waterleaf weighted by
its hardened raindrop surface.
72   The paper-mould's similarly

once unsolid waspnest-blue, snow-
white, or seashell-gray rags, seen through, show
    sheepcotes, turkey-
mills, acorns, and anvils. "Stones grow,"
77 then stop, and so
    do gardens. "Plants grow and live; men
    grow and live and think." *Utilizey la poste
aerienne,* trade will follow
81   the telephone. The post's jerky

cancellings ink the stamp, relet-
tering stiltedly, as a puppet-
    acrobat walks
about with high steps on his net,
86 an alphabet
    of words and animals where the
    wire-embedded watermark's more integral
expressiveness had first set
90   its alabaster effigy.

[62]

Marianne Moore

In bark silverer than the swan,
esparto grass, or so-called Titan
   parchment tougher
than Hercules' lion-skin — Span-
95 ish, Umbrian,
   eastern, open, and jewelled crowns,
   corroborate the dolphin, crane, and ox; sealed
with wax by a pelican
99   studying affectionately

a nest's three-in-one cartwheel tri-
legged face. "For those we love, live and die"
   the motto says.
And we do. Part pelican, I,
104 doubting the high-
   way's wide giant trivia where
   three roads meet in artificial openness,
am obliged to justify
108   outspoken cordiality.

Firm-feathered juniper springing
from difficult ground, the sky trembling
   with power, the rain
falling upon the bird singing,
113 modest printing,
   on honest paper properly
   trimmed, are gifts addressed to memory, and a
gift is permanent, shining
117   like the juniper's trinity

[63]

of spines. An unburdensomely
worthy officer of charity,
   the evergreen
with awlshaped leaves in whorls of three —
successively
   firm. "On the first day of Christmas
   my true love he sent unto me, part of a
bough of a juniper-tree,"
      javelin-ed consecutively.

Marianne Moore

WALKING-STICKS AND PAPERWEIGHTS AND WATERMARKS

PRESENTATIONS:

Poetry 49 (November 1936): 59–64.
What Are Years. New York: Macmillan, 1941: 10–14.

TEXTUAL VARIANTS 1936–1941:

ti. *Po* "Walking-Sticks and Paperweights and Watermarks" | *WAY* "Walking-Sticks and Paper-Weights and Water Marks"

The revisions to this poem are too extensive to be enumerated by line; instead I have provided a side-by-side comparison, with material unique to each poem marked in bold.

FIGURE 6: "'For those we love, live and die' the motto says."
"Walking-Sticks and Paperweights and Watermarks" (1936), ll.101–102

Walking among sceptre-headed
weeds and daisies swayed by wind**, t**hey said,
    "**Don't** scatter your
stick, on account of the **souls**." Led
from sun-spotted
    paths, we went "where leafy trees meet
    overhead and noise of traffic is unknown"—
the mind exhilarated
        by life all round, so stirringly

alive. **The** root**-handled** cudgel
with the bark left on, the woodbine smell-
    ing of the rain,
the very stones**, have** life. Little
scars on church-bell
    tongues put there by the Devil's claws—
    authentic phantoms, ghosts, and witches, transformed
into an invisible
        fabric of inconsistency

**motheaten by self-subtractives—
now as outright murderers and thieves,**
    thrive openly.
An epigraph before it leaves
the wax, receives
    to give, and giving must itself
    receive, "difficulty is ordained to check
poltroons," and courage achieves
        despaired of ends. **Oppositely**

jointed against indecision,
the three legs of the triskelion
    meeting in the
middle between triangles, run
in unison
    without assistance. Yet, trudging
    on two legs that move contradictorily,
irked by ghosts and witches, one
        does not fear to ask for beauty

1941 *What Are Years*

Jointed against indecision,
the three legs of the triskelion
    meeting in the
middle between triangles, run
in unison,
    self-assisted. And yet, trudging
    on two legs that move contradictorily,
despite ghosts and witches, one
        does not fear to ask for beauty.

Stepped glass has been made in Ireland;
they still have blackthorn walking-sticks, and
    flax and linen
and paper-mills; and reprimand
you if you stand
    your stick on such and such a spot.
    You must keep to the path "on account of the
souls." And all can understand
        how centralizing loyalty

shapes matter as a die is hid
while used; and that such power, unavid
    since secure, can
mold an at first fluid solid
glass weight. Amid
    the wax the seal is safe. Also
    as the water mark's translucence clearly seen
can fascinate, the vivid-
        ly white flower attracts one lightly

brushing against sceptre-headed
weeds and daisies swayed by wind. [They said,
    "**Do not** scatter
your stick, on account of the **dead.**"]
The pathway led
    into woods "where leafy trees meet
    overhead and noise of traffic is unknown"—
the mind exhilarated
        by life all round, so stirringly

that is power **devoid of** fear.
A bold outspoken gentleman, cheer-
    ful, plodding, to-
the-point, used to the atmosphere
41   of work—**who here**
    appropriate to the thought of
    permanence, says, "this is my taste, it might not
be another man's"—**makes clear**
45   **that stark s**incere **unflattery,**

sine cera, is both farthest
from self-defensiveness and nearest;
    as when a seal
without haste, slowly is impressed
50   and forms a nest
    on which the raised device reversed,
    shows round. It must have been an able workman,
studious and self-possessed,
54   a liker of solidity,

who gave **a** greenish Waterford
glass **fool's cap** with summit curled down toward
    itself as the
glass grew, the look of tempered sword-
59   steel**, and** three-ore-d
    fishscale-burnished antimony-
    tin-and-lead's smoky water-drop type-metal
smoothness emery-armored
63   against rust. Its subdued glossy

splendor leaps out at the eye as
form dramatizes thought, in the glass
    witchball **and** air-
twist cane. This paperweight, in mass
68   a stone, surpass-
    ing it in tint, enlarges the
    fine chain-lines **in** the **waterleaf** weighted by
its hardened raindrop surface.
72   The paper-mould's similarly

alive. **Fancy's rude** root cudgel
with the bark left on, the woodbine smell-
 of the rain,
the very stones **had** life. Little
scars on churchbell-
 tongues, put there by the Devil's claws,
 **and other forms of negativeness need but
be expressed and visible,**
 to prove their unauthority.

**Patience, with its superlatives,
firmness and loyalty and faith, gives
 intensive fruit.
As a device** before it leaves
the wax, receives
 to give, and giving must itself
 receive, "difficulty is ordained to check
poltroons," and courage achieves
 despaired-of ends **inversely,—**

mute with power **and strong with** fear.
A bold outspoken gentleman, cheer-
 ful, plodding, to-
the-point, used to the atmosphere
of work**, and there-
 fore author of the permanent,**
 says **modestly,** "This is my taste, it might not
be another man's." Sincere
 unforced unconscious honesty,

sine cera, **can be furthest**
from self-defensiveness and nearest;
 as when a seal
without haste, slowly is impressed,
and forms a nest
 on which the raised device reversed,
 shows round. It must have been an able workman,
humorous and self-possessed,
 a liker of solidity,

once unsolid **waspnest**-blue, **snow-**
white, **or seashell-gray rags,** seen through, show
    sheepcotes, turkey-
mills, acorns, and anvils. "Stones grow,"
then stop, and so
    do gardens. "Plants **grow and live;** men
      grow and live and think." *Utilizey la poste*
aerienne, **trade will follow**
        the telephone. The post's jerky

cancellings ink the stamp, relet-
tering stiltedly, as a puppet-
    acrobat walks
about with high steps on his net,
an alphabet
    of words and animals where the
      wire-embedded watermark's more integral
expressiveness had first set
        its alabaster effigy.

In bark silverer than **the** swan,
esparto grass, or so-called Titan
    parchment tougher
than Hercules' lion-skin—Span-
ish, Umbrian,
    eastern, open, **and** jewelled crowns,
      corroborate the dolphin, crane, **and** ox; sealed
with wax **by** a pelican
        studying affectionately

a nest's three-in-one **cartwheel** tri-
legged face. "For those we love, live and die"
    the motto **says.**
And we do. Part pelican, **I,**
doubting the high-
    way's **wide giant** trivia where
      three roads meet **in artificial openness,**
am obliged to justify
        outspoken cordiality.

1941

who gave **this** greenish Waterford
glass **weight** with **the** summit curled down toward
    itself as the
glass grew, the look of tempered sword-
steel; **of** three-ore-d
    fishscale-burnished antimony-
        lead-and-tin smoky water-drop type-metal
smoothness emery-armored
    against rust. Its subdued glossy

splendor leaps out at the eye as
the light does not shine even from glass
    air-twist cane**s, or**
witchball**s.** This paperweight, in mass
a stone, surpass-
    ing it in tint, enlarges the
        fine chain-lines **on** the **letter-flap** weighted by
its hardened rain-drop surface.
    The paper-mold's similarly

at first unsolid blue**s, yellow-**
white**s and lavenders, when** seen through, show
    leopards, eagles,
quills, acorns and anvils. "Stones grow,"
as volcano-
    sides and quartz-mines prove. "Plants **feel? Men**
        think." "Airmail is quick." "Save rags, bones, metals." Hopes
are harvest when deeds follow
    words postmarked "Dig for victory."

Postmark behests are clearer than
the water marks beneath,—than ox, swan,
    crane**, or** dolphin,
than eastern, open, jewelled, Span-
ish, Umbrian
    crown,—**as symbols of endurance.**
    And making the envelope secure, the sealed
wax **reveals** a pelican
    studying affectionately

1936

Firm-feathered juniper springing
from difficult ground, the sky trembling
　　　with power, the rain
falling upon the bird singing,
modest printing,
　　　on honest paper properly
　　　trimmed, are gifts addressed to memory, and a
gift is permanent, shining
　　　　　　like the juniper's trinity

of spines. An unburdensomely
worthy officer of charity,
　　　the evergreen
with awlshaped leaves in whorls of three—
successively
　　　firm. "On the first day of Christmas
　　　my true love he sent unto me, part of a
bough of a juniper-tree,"
　　　　　　javelin-ed consecutively.

1941

the nest's three-in-one **upturned** tri-
form face. "For those we love, live and die"
    the motto **reads.**
**The pelican's community
of throats,** the high-
    way's trivia **or crow's-foot** where
    three roads meet, **the fugue, the** awl-**leafed juniper's**
whorls of three, **objectify**
        welded divisiveness. Of the

juniper **that in balladry
has been kept green, the fugue's three times three**
    reiterat-
ed **chain of interactingly
linked harmony,**
    says "On the first day of Christmas
    my true love he sent unto me, part of a
bough of a juniper-tree,"
        repeated to infinity.

FIGURES 7 & 8: "Oppositely//jointed against indecision,/the three legs of the triskelion/meeting in the/middle between triangles, run/in unison/without assistance."
"Walking-Sticks and Paperweights and Watermarks" (1936), ll. 27–33

May 20, 1932

Shaw's play "Too Good to be True". Correspondent for the London Times, Boston selected as keynote of the play these lines: "All I know is that I must find the way of life for myself and for all of us, or we shall surely perish. Meanwhile my gift has possession of me. I must preach and preach and preach, no matter how late the hour, or short the day, no matter whether I have nothing to say."

June 11, 1932

From The Illus. London News of Dec. 2, 1932 Frank Slavis on "John Speed Cartographer" b. 1552

John Speed's erudition sometimes makes him a trifle owlish, & legend & fact are as often as not all one in his eyes, but in this he is but the child of his time. Of Cambridgeshire he says: "the fenny surcharged with waters;.... upon the East bank of the river Came the Muses have built their most sacred Seat, where with plenteous increase they have continued for these many hundred years." How much nicer than to read — "On the bank of the Cam is the University town of Cambridge

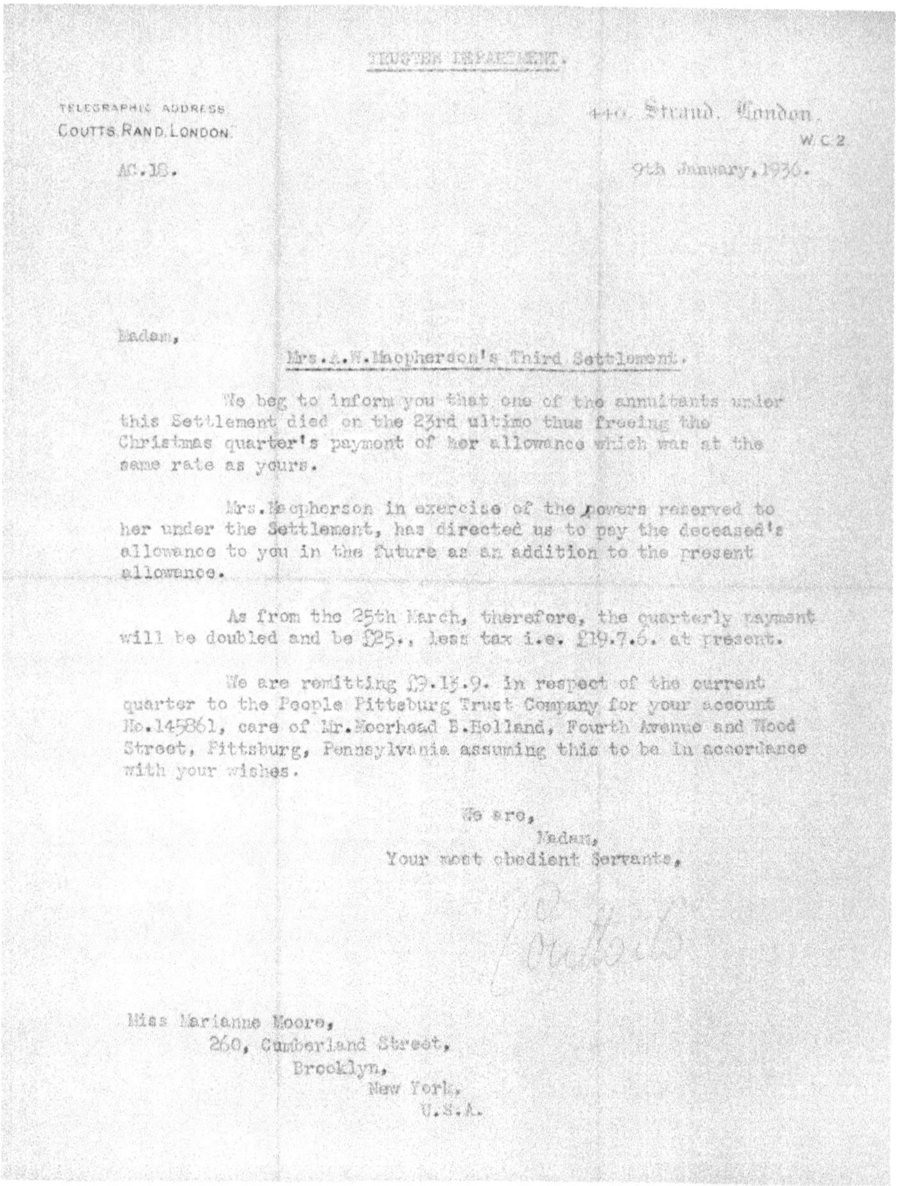

TRUSTEE DEPARTMENT.

TELEGRAPHIC ADDRESS:
COUTTS, RAND, LONDON.

440, Strand, London.
W.C.2

AC.18.

9th January, 1936.

Madam,

Mrs. A. W. Macpherson's Third Settlement.

We beg to inform you that one of the annuitants under this Settlement died on the 23rd ultimo thus freeing the Christmas quarter's payment of her allowance which war at the same rate as yours.

Mrs. Macpherson in exercise of the powers reserved to her under the Settlement, has directed us to pay the deceased's allowance to you in the future as an addition to the present allowance.

As from the 25th March, therefore, the quarterly payment will be doubled and be £25., less tax i.e. £19.7.6. at present.

We are remitting £9.13.9. in respect of the current quarter to the People Pittsburg Trust Company for your account No. 145861, care of Mr. Moorhead B. Holland, Fourth Avenue and Wood Street, Pittsburg, Pennsylvania assuming this to be in accordance with your wishes.

We are,
Madam,
Your most obedient Servants,

Miss Marianne Moore,
260, Cumberland Street,
Brooklyn,
New York,
U.S.A.

FIGURE 9: "once unsolid waspnest-blue, snow-/white, or seashell-gray rags, seen through, show/[...] turkey-/mills" / "Walking-Sticks and Paperweights and Watermarks" (1936), ll. 73–76

POEMS

By MARIANNE MOORE

Four Quartz Crystal Clocks

There are four vibrators, the world's exactest clocks;
    and these quartz time-pieces that tell
time intervals to other clocks,
    these worksless clocks work well;
and all four, independently the
    same are there, in the cool Bell
        Laboratory time

vault. Checked by a comparator with Arlington,
    they punctualize the "radio,
cinema, and press," — a group the
    Giraudoux truth-bureau
of hoped-for accuracy has termed
    "instruments of truth." We know —
        as Jean Giraudoux says

certain Arabs have not heard—that Napoleon
    is dead; that a quartz prism when
the temperature changes, feels
    the change and that the then
electrified alternate edges
    oppositely charged, threaten
        careful timing; so that

Kenyon Review 2 (Summer 1940): 284–285.

this water-clear "crystal" as the Greeks used to say,
    this "clear ice" must be kept at the
same coolness. Repetition, with
    the scientist, should be
synonymous with accuracy.
    The lemur-student can see
        that an aye-aye is not

an angwan-tíbo, potto, or loris.   The sea-
    side burden should not embarrass
the bell-boy with the buoy-ball
    endeavoring to pass
hotel patronesses; nor could a
    practised ear confuse the glass
        eyes for taxidermists

with eye-glasses from the optometrist.   And as
    Meridian 7 one-two
one-two gives, each fifteenth second
    in the same voice, the new
data — "The time will be" so and so —
    you realize that "when you
        hear the signal," you'll be

hearing Jupiter or jour pater, the day god —
    the salvaged son of Father Time —
telling the cannibal Chronos
    (eater of his proxime,
newborn progeny) that punctual-
    ity is not now a crime.

FOUR QUARTZ CRYSTAL CLOCKS

PRESENTATIONS:

Kenyon Review 2 (Summer 1940): 284–285.
What Are Years. New York: Macmillan, 1941: 37–38.

TEXTUAL VARIANTS 1940–1941:

6. *Ken* same [...] there,| *WAY* same, [...] there
10. *Ken* cinema, and press," | *WAY* cinéma," and "presse,"
22. *Ken* "crystal" | *WAY* crystal
31. *Ken* bell-boy | *WAY* bell-buoy [*]
34. *Ken* practised | *WAY* practiced
37–8. *Ken* Meridian 7 one-two/one-two | *WAY* MEridian-7 1, 2/1, 2
46. *Ken* proxime, | *WAY* proxime
48. *Ken* not now | *WAY* not

* This line has a vexed history. As noted here, the Macmillan edition of *What Are Years* makes nonsense of the poem's thirty-first line by printing "the bell-buoy with the buoy-ball," a mistake for which Elizabeth Bishop vowed she would "never forgive" them (*One Art* 104). Bishop was especially sensitive because she considered it "[*her*] line" (104), one of which she felt "extremely proud" (89). Thirty years later Bishop was still not at ease about it, noting in her essay "Efforts of Affection" that Moore had (uncharacteristically) used the phrase, which originated with Bishop, without attribution (*Prose* 141).

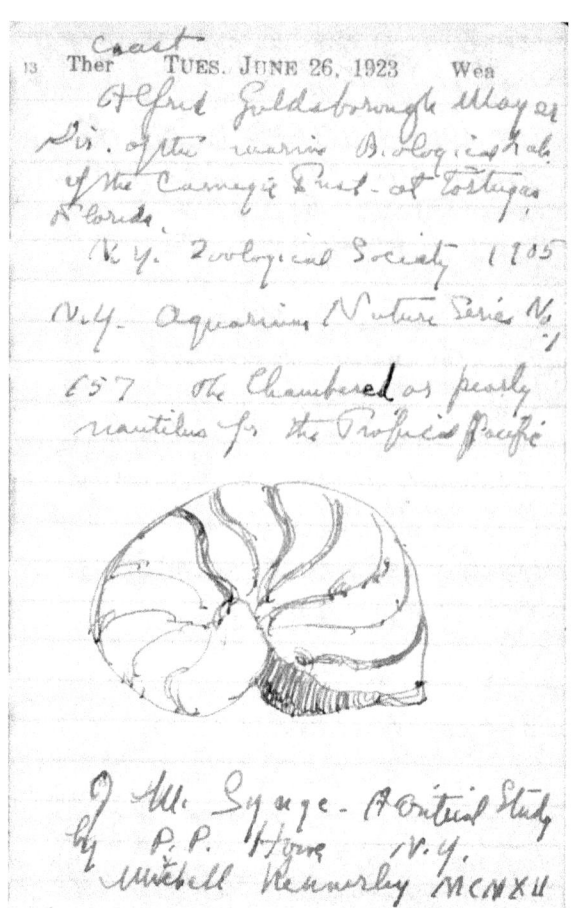

FIGURE 10: "her perishable/souvenir of hope"
"A Glass-Ribbed Nest" (1940), ll. 8–9

A Glass-Ribbed Nest

For authorities whose hopes
are shaped by mercenaries?
　Writers entrapped by
　teatime fame and by
commuters' comforts? Not for these
　the paper nautilus
constructs her thin glass shell.

　Giving her perishable
souvenir of hope, a dull
　white outside and smooth-
　edged inner side as
glossy as the sea, the watchful
　animal takes charge of
　it herself and scarcely

　leaves it till the eggs are hatched.
Buried eight-fold in her eight
　arms, for she is in
　a sense a devil-
fish, her glass ramshorn-cradled freight
　is hid but is not crushed.
　As Hercules, bitten

by a crab loyal to the hydra,
was hindered to succeed,
　the intensively
　watched eggs coming from
the shell, free it when they are freed,—
　leaving its wasp-nest flaws
　of white on white, and close-

Kenyon Review 2 (Summer 1940): 287–288.

laid Ionic chiton-folds
like the lines in the mane of
　a Parthenon horse,
　round which the arms had
wound themselves as if they knew love
　is the only fortress
35　strong enough to trust to.

A GLASS-RIBBED NEST

PRESENTATIONS:

Kenyon Review 2 (Summer 1940): 287–288.
Life and Letters Today 26 (September 1940): 244–245.
What Are Years. New York: Macmillan, 1941: 44–45.

TEXTUAL VARIANTS 1940–1941:

ti. *Ken, Li* "A Glass-Ribbed Nest" | *WAY* "The Paper Nautilus"

3. *Ken, WAY* entrapped | *Li* ensnared
4. *Ken, WAY* teatime | *Li* tea-time
11. *Ken* side as | *Li, WAY* surface
12–5. *Ken* watchful
      animal takes charge of
      it **herself and** scarcely

      leav**es** it till |

      Li watchful**,**
      the tense mother, clutches
      it**,** scarcely leav**ing or**

      eat**ing** till |

      WAY watchful
      maker of it guards it
      day and night; she scarcely

      eat**s until**

26. *Ken* shell, [...] freed,— *Li* shell, [...] freed— | *WAY* shell [...] freed,—

What Are Years?

What is our innocence,
what is our guilt? All are
   naked, none is safe. And whence
is courage: the unanswered question,
the resolute doubt,—
dumbly calling, deafly listening — that
in misfortune, even death,
   encourages others
   and in its defeat, stirs

the soul to be strong? He
sees deep and is glad, who
   accedes to mortality
and in his imprisonment, rises
upon himself as
the sea in a chasm, struggling to be
free and unable to be,
   in its surrendering
   finds its continuing.

So he who strongly feels,
behaves. The very bird,
   grown taller as he sings, steels
his form straight up though he is captive.
His mighty singing
says; satisfaction is a lowly
thing, how pure a thing is joy.
   This is mortality,
   this is eternity.

Kenyon Review 2 (Summer 1940): 286.

WHAT ARE YEARS?

PRESENTATIONS:

Kenyon Review 2 (Summer 1940): 286.
What Are Years. New York: Macmillan, 1941: 1.

TEXTUAL VARIANTS 1940–1941:

22–3. *Ken* up though [...] captive./His | *WAY* uThough [...] captive,/his
24. *Ken* says; | *WAY* says,

is it because a man is left alone,
or is it progress or poverty that is the proof of wrong?
that leaves him naked to his memories...."

That was what she meant and if I could find the letter,
it would be there: she said it was wonderful
to see him almost happy, even in bad weather,
nor did he worry about his father's grave that he could
    not find,
or whether he had died at midnight or as the sun rose
    red
on a grey-skied morning.

HORACE GREGORY

RIGORISTS

"WE SAW REINDEER
browsing," a friend who'd been in Lapland, said;
"finding their own food; they are adapted   3

    to scant *reino*
or pasture, yet they can run eleven
miles in fifty minutes; the feet spread when   6

    the snow is soft,
and act as snow-shoes. They are rigorists
even if cutwork exteriorists   9

    of Lapland and
Siberia elaborate the trace
or saddle-girth with saw-tooth leather lace.   12

Life and Letters Today 26 (September 1940): 243–244.

            One looked at us
with a firm face part brown, part white; a queen
15   of alpine flowers. Santa Claus' reindeer, seen

            at last, had grey-
brown fur, with a neck like edelweiss or
18   lion's foot—leontopodium more

            exactly." And
this candalabrum-headed ornament
21   for a place where ornaments are scarce—sent

            to Alaska—
was a gift preventing the extinction
24   of the Esquimaux; a stubborn race, gone

            but for it—for
it, imported by a missionary,
27   fervent man. Its firm face is augury.

                    MARIANNE MOORE

A GLASS-RIBBED NEST

FOR AUTHORITIES WHOSE hopes
are shaped by mercenaries?
    Writers ensnared by
    tea-time fame and by
commuters' comforts? Not for these
    the paper nautilus
constructs her thin glass shell.

RIGORISTS

PRESENTATIONS:

Life and Letters Today 26 (September 1940): 243–244.
Furioso 1 (Summer 1941): 23–24
What Are Years. New York: Macmillan, 1941: 2–3.

TEXTUAL VARIANTS 1940–1941:

2. *Li* said; | *Fu, WAY* said:
9. *Li* even if cutwork exteriorists | *Fu, WAY* however handsomely cutwork artists
12. *Li, WAY* or | *Fu* and
14. *Li* a [...] white; | *Fu, WAY* its [...] white,—
16. *Li* grey | *Fu, WAY* gray
18. *Li* foot—leontopodium | *Fu, WAY* foot,—*leontopodium*
20. *Li, Fu* candalabrum-headed | *WAY* candelabrum-headed
21. *Li* scarce— | *Fu, WAY* scarce,
22. *Li* Alaska— | *Fu, WAY* Alaska,
24-7. *Li* Esquim**aux; a stubborn** race, **gone**

> **but for it—for**
> **it, imported by a missionary,**
> **fervent** man. **Its firm** face **is augury.** |

Fu, WAY Esquim**o. The battle was won**

> **by a quiet** man,
> Sheldon Jackson, evangel to that race
> whose reprieve he read in the reindeer's face.

MARIANNE MOORE

LIGHT IS SPEECH

*One can say more of sunlight
    than of speech; but speech
    and light, each
aiding each—when French—
have not disgraced that still un-
extirpated adjective.
Yes light is speech. Free frank
impartial sunlight, moonlight,
starlight, lighthouse light,
    are language. The Creach'h
    d'Ouessant light-
house on its defenceless dot of
rock, is the descendant of Voltaire*

*whose flaming justice saved a
    man already harmed;
    of unarmed
Montaigne whose balance,
maintained despite the bandit's
hardness, lit remorse's saving
spark; of Emile Littré,
philology's determined,
ardent eight-volume
    Hippocrates-charmed
    editor. A
man on fire, a scientist of
freedoms, was firm Maximilien*

*Paul Emile Littré. England
    guarded by the sea,
    we with re-
enforced Bartholdy's
Liberty holding up her
torch beside the port, hear France
demand, " 'Tell me the truth,
especially when it is
    unpleasant.' " And we
    cannot but reply,
"The word France means
enfranchisement; means one who can
'animate whoever thinks of her.' "*

Decision 1 (March 1941): 26.

LIGHT IS SPEECH

PRESENTATIONS:

Decision 1 (March 1941): 26.
What Are Years. New York: Macmillan, 1941: 4–5.

TEXTUAL VARIANTS 1941:

12. *De* defenceless | *WAY* defenseless
14. *De* saved | *WAY* reached
20. *De* Emile | *WAY* Émile
27. *De* Emile | *WAY* Émile

        exactly." And
this candalabrum-headed ornament
for a place where ornaments are scarce, sent

        to Alaska,
was a gift preventing the extinction
of the Esquimo. The battle was won

        by a quiet man,
Sheldon Jackson, evangel to that race
whose reprieve he read in the reindeer's face.

SPENSER'S IRELAND

has not altered;—
        the kindest place I've never been,
        the greenest place I've never seen.
Every name is a tune.
Denunciations do not affect
        the culprit;   nor blows, but it
is torture to him to not be spoken to.
They're natural,—
        the coat, like Venus'
mantle lined with stars,
buttoned close at the neck,—the
        sleeves new from disuse.

It was Irish;
        a match not a marriage was made
        when my great great grandmother'd said
with native genius for
disunion, "although your suitor be
        perfection,   one objection
is enough; he is not
Irish." Outwitting
        the fairies, befriending the furies,
whoever again
and again says, "I'll never
        give in," never sees

Page Twenty-four

           that you're not free
               until you've been made captive by
               supreme belief,—credulity
           you say? When large dainty
           fingers tremblingly divide the wings
30   of the fly   for mid-July
           with a needle and wrap it with peacock-tail,
           or tie wool and
                     buzzard's wing, their pride,
           like the enchanter's
           is in care, not madness. It's
36   faithful hands divide

           flax for damask
               that when bleached by Irish weather
               has the silvered chamois-leather
           water-tightness of a
           skin. Twisted torcs and gold new-moon-shaped
42   lunulae   aren't jewelry
           like the purple-coral fuschia-tree's. If Eire—
           "the guillemot
                     so neat" and the hen
           of the heath and "the
           linnet spinet-sweet" — bespeak
48   relentlessness, then

           they are to me
               like enchanted Earl Gerald who
               changed himself into a stag, to
           a great green-eyed cat of
           the mountain. Discommodity makes
54   them invis   ible; they've dis-
           appeared. The Irish say "your trouble is their
           trouble and your
                     joy their joy?" I wish
           I could believe it;
           I am troubled, I'm dissat-
60   isfied, I'm Irish.

                                        MARIANNE MOORE

                                        Page Twenty-five

SPENSER'S IRELAND

PRESENTATIONS:

Furioso 1 (Summer 1941): 24–25.
What Are Years. New York: Macmillan, 1941: 34–36.

TEXTUAL VARIANTS 1941:

13–24. *WAY* stanza inserted; see 48
35–6.   *Fu* It's/faithful | 47–8. *WAY* Con-/curring
43.   *Fu* fuschia-tree's |55. *WAY* fuchsia-tree's
44–5.   *Fu* "the [...] neat" 56–7. *WAY* the [...] neat
46–7.   *Fu* "the/linnet spinet-sweet" | 58–9. *WAY* the/linnet spinet-sweet |
55–7.   *Fu* "your trouble is their/trouble and your/joy their joy?" | 67–9.*WAY* your trouble is their/trouble and your/joy their joy?

rights things would have been very different. I have inherited her resentment against England, taking part with all those who have carried Empire on their shoulders and been given slums to live in for their pains. I have always hated the English ruling class and as a result feel that, in many ways, whatever England gets now is a just retribution. But, at heart, I am in great part proud of my English blood and so you have the whole picture. Perhaps it should be added that my contempt for and distrust of T. S. Eliot and all he does and says comes from the feeling I have that he and others like him have allied themselves with that part of the English character which unless it is cleansed by an economic and therefore spiritual hurricane will destroy that which I, in a way very different from theirs, profoundly love.—W. C. WILLIAMS, June 1, 1941.

Marianne Moore

HE "DIGESTETH HARDE YRON"

Although the aepyornis
or roc that lives in Madagascar, and
   the moa are extinct,
     the camel-sparrow, linked
with them in size—the large sparrow
Xenophon saw walking by
   a stream—was and is
     a symbol of justice.

This bird watches his chicks with
a maternal concentration, after
   he has sat on the eggs
     at night six weeks, his legs
their only weapon of defense.
He is swifter than a horse;
   he has a foot hard
     as a hoof; the leopard

is not more suspicious. How
could he, prized for plumes and eggs and young,
   even as a riding-   used
     beast, respect men hiding

actorlike in ostrich-skins, with
the right hand making the neck move
   as if alive and
     from a bag the left hand

strewing grain, that ostriches
might be decoyed and killed! Yes this is he
   whose plume was anciently
     the plume of justice; he
whose comic duckling head on its
great neck, revolves with compass-
   needle nervousness,
     when he stands guard, in S-

like foragings as he is
preening the down on his leaden-skinned back.
   The egg piously shown
     as Leda's very own
from which Castor and Pollux hatched,
was an ostrich-egg. And what
   could have been more fit
     for the Chinese lawn it

grazed on, as a gift to an
emperor who admired strange birds, than this
   one who builds his mud-made
     nest in dust yet will wade
in lake or sea till only the
head shows. A nervous restless
   bird that flees at sight
     of danger, he feigns flight

to save his chicks, decoying
his decoyers; never known to hide his
   head in sand, yet lagging
     when he must, and dragging
an as-if-wounded wing. The friend
of hippotigers and wild
   asses, it is as
     though schooled by them he was

        the best of the unflying
        pegasi, since the Greeks "caught a few wild
           asses but no ostrich;"
            quadrupedlike bird which
        flies on feet not wings,—his moth-silk
        plumage wilted by his speed;
           mobile wings and tail
            behaving as a sail.

        Six hundred ostrich-brains served
        at one banquet, the ostrich-plume-tipped tent
           and desert spear, jewel-
            gorgeous ugly egg-shell
        goblets, eight pairs of ostriches
        in harness, dramatize a
           meaning always missed
            by the externalist.

        The power of the visible
        is the invisible; as even where
           no tree of freedom grows,
            so-called brute courage knows.
        Heroism is exhausting, yet
        it contradicts a greed that
           did not wisely spare
            the harmless solitaire

        or great auk in its grandeur;
        unsolicitude having swallowed up
           all giant birds but an
            alert gargantuan
        little-winged, magnificently
        speedy running-bird. This one
           remaining rebel
            is the sparrow-camel.

HE "DIGESTETH HARDE YRON"

PRESENTATIONS:

Partisan Review 8 (July-August 1941): 312–314.
What Are Years. New York: Macmillan, 1941: 6–9.

TEXTUAL VARIANTS 1941:

2. *PaR* lives | *WAY* lived

ANNOTATED LIST OF ILLUSTRATIONS

FRONT COVER: Marianne Moore. Persimmons. Watercolor. Sketchbook 1253/8. [1936-1937], XIII:03:10. Marianne Moore Collection, Rosenbach Museum & Library, Philadelphia. This sketch of persimmons, dated November 15, 1936, is an echo of a thought Moore expressed in a 1932 letter to Kenneth Burke. In the context of an ongoing discussion about labor economics Moore wrote: "at the risk of making myself look worse than I am, I confess to buying butter and potatoes at the A.& P. though my small grocer whom I occasionally patronize, goes out of business; and to writing a poem on a persimmon let us say instead of joining with our capitalist friends in handing out the local dole..." (*Selected Letters* 283).

FIGURE 1 (page 82): Marianne Moore. Sketch of a petrel. Moore notebook 1250/6, VII:02:02. Marianne Moore Collection, Rosenbach Museum & Library, Philadelphia. Moore made this sketch in the reading notebook she kept in the 1930s (although the page itself bears an earlier printed date). On the page facing the sketch one may read her notes on an article from the 24 January 1931 issue of the *London Illustrated News*:

> X-ray photos as aides to science's
> studies of antarctic birds
> The structure of a bird which in
> contrast to the penguin is nearly
> always on the wing: the Wilson
> Petrel—an x-ray photograph
> weighs only one ounce, & has a total
> wing-spread of 15 inches-
> —— Penguins are an ancient
> order of birds, & consequently
> show primitive characters
> They are backward rather than
> degenerate

The sketch itself is a copy of the petrel x-ray to which the first half of the paragraph refers; on the same page of the article there are x-ray photographs of prions and penguins as well. The lines she quotes about penguins became the source for lines 41–2 of the 1932 "The Student."

FIGURE 2 (page 90): Marianne Moore. Flowers. Watercolor. Sketchbook 1253/8 [1936-1937], XIII:03:10. Marianne Moore Collection, Rosenbach Museum & Library, Philadelphia. This sketch of mimosa flowers (a botanical identification made by the editor, as the sketch itself is untitled) is one of a number of sketches Moore made while visiting her brother Warner in Norfolk, Virginia, in the summer of 1936 (just after the publication of *The Pangolin and Other Verse*, in which the "Old Dominion" series appears).

FIGURE 3 (page 100): Sketch of Thomas Orwin's printer's mark by Marianne Moore. Moore notebook 1250/6, VII:02:02. Marianne Moore Collection, Rosenbach Museum & Library, Philadelphia.

FIGURE 4 (page 100): Thomas Orwin's printer's mark. In McKerrow. This printer's mark appears on the frontispiece of the 1590 edition of Thomas Lodge's *Rosalynde*. The notes to *What Are Years* cite it as the source for the final lines in "Smooth Gnarled Crape Myrtle:" "And what of /clasped hands that swear, 'By Peace/Plenty; as/by Wisdom Peace.' Alas!" (35). Moore's interest in the visual composition of the mark is evident in the drawings, made by George Plank in consultation with Moore, for her 1936 *The Pangolin and Other Verse*: two of them allude to the clasped hands at its center (see *A-Quiver* 127–9).

FIGURE 5 (page 106): Marianne Moore. Pomegranates. Watercolor. 2006.4482. Marianne Moore Collection, Rosenbach Museum & Library, Philadelphia. This painting is undated, but its strong compositional similarity to another painting (of pale-and deep-purple petunias) in the archive suggests she may have made it in 1932. Pomegranates appear in both "Half Deity" and "Virginia Britannia," as well as in a letter (14 August 1935) Moore wrote to George Plank describing her inspiration for the latter poem:

> I have been follied into another effort—a kind of commentary on Virginia.... It deals with Jamestown church-tower ruin and table tombstones, and Captain John Smith's coat of arms, (a Turk's head and an ostrich with a horseshoe in its beak), dwarf box-edged flower beds, ivy arbors and lead statuary, saddle horses, hounds, raccoons, owls, French furniture, and so on; the pomegranate and African violet also. (*Selected Letters* 352)

FIGURE 6 (page 129): Wax seal on envelope. Autograph letter from Hildegarde Watson to Mary W. Moore. Rochester, 26 October 1935. V:70:02. Marianne Moore Collection, Rosenbach Museum & Library, Philadelphia. Hildegarde Watson, wife of *Dial* co-owner Sibley Watson, was a close friend and prolific correspondent of Moore's from the mid-1930s on. She also corresponded with Moore's mother; in a letter to Watson (28 June 1936, Berg Collection, New York Public Library, hereafter cited as Berg) Mrs. Moore remarked on an especially successful impress of Watson's characteristic seal: "Your fine print of the pelican seal ought to be studied with a microscope. How could you make it so perfect? And too it is a beautiful thing. I regard it as a special gift." Moore refers to the seal in both of her published versions of "Walking-Sticks and Paperweights and Watermarks," as well in a draft version where she refers to it as "What perquisite so// portraitlike, or so possessed/of depth and curiosity" (Rosenbach). Watson noted the presence of her seal in the poem in a letter to Moore (28 October 1936) written after "Walking-Sticks" appeared in *Poetry*: "Your poem is very beautiful.... The pelican seal is so fine a picture" (Berg).

FIGURES 7 AND 8 (page 138–39): Mary W. Moore. Grapefruit label and sketch. Notebook 1250/19, VII:03:08. Marianne Moore Collection, Rosenbach Museum & Library, Philadelphia. This image is in a notebook Mary Warner Moore kept in 1932, when Warner Moore was stationed in Samoa (habitat of, among other things, special "Samoan grapefruit"). "Pago-Pago," or simply "Pago," was one of the family nicknames for Warner at the time; above the grapefruit label Mrs. Moore has copied "'Fidelity, Courage, Purpose Indomitable.' May 18, 1932. From Pago's acc't-book in college." Just below this inscription and to the right of the label Mrs. Moore pasted in, at a later time, two small drawings of marionettes and wrote beneath them "From Pago, April 11, 1936." On the facing page Mrs. Moore has sketched a second triskelion. Moore and her mother's shared interest in the triskelion, with its strong association with Warner's work abroad, may suggest it had resonance for them as a symbol of their own tripartite family unity, and their collective pride in "run[ning] in unison without assistance" ("Walking-Sticks [1936]," ll.31–3).

FIGURE 9 (page 140): Coutts Trustee Department. Typed letter signed to Marianne Moore. London, 9 January 1936. XI:02:05. Marianne Moore Collection, Rosenbach Museum & Library, Philadelphia. Mrs. A.W. Macpherson, whose "Third Settlement" is the subject of this letter, is Moore's friend the writer, publisher, and patron of the arts Bryher (see xxx, n.1). In a letter to Moore also dated 9 January 1936 Bryher informed Moore of a forthcoming addition to the annuity she had already arranged for Moore's support. She claimed that the addition was an inheritance from a deceased elderly relative of Perdita Schaffner (the poet H.D.'s daughter and Bryher's ward) that only an American citizen could receive. Bryher claimed:

any correspondence about this money must be addressed to Messrs Coutts...and not to me, nor must you attempt in any way to return any of same to me, or I should be liable to heavy penalties over here. You see, I know from experience what you are like. Had the death occurred in England, you would not have benefitted, as it is, you do. And I can't help this, nor do anything else about it. It is down in black and white on a piece of parchment duly reposing in Coutts bank. (Rosenbach)

Moore's response to this gift was characteristically complex, but one trace of it may be found in "Walking-Sticks and Paperweights and Watermarks." That poem's seventy-fifth and -sixth lines list a number of watermarks: "sheepcotes, turkey-/mills, acorns, and anvils." In a letter dated 7 November 1936 Moore tells Bryher that "I had mentioned in it—somewhat for your eye—Original Old Turkey Mill, the watermark in the Coutts Bank blue stationery" (*Selected Letters* 370).

FIGURE 10 (page 144): Marianne Moore. Sketch of a nautilus. Moore notebook 1250/6, VII:02:02. Marianne Moore Collection, Rosenbach Museum & Library, Philadelphia. This sketch, made in a notebook of Moore's, is of a photograph of a nautilus shell on page 157 of Alfred Goldsborough Mayor's *Sea-Shore Life: The Invertebrates of the New York Coast*. The printed date on the notebook page is June 26, 1923, but Moore was in fact using the book in the 1930s. The notes surrounding the sketch show that she made it between 10 September and 24 December 1933. This date is notable because it demonstrates Moore's long-standing interest in the nautilus, pre-dating by four years Elizabeth Bishop's and Louise Crane's gift to her of a nautilus shell, and by seven years her poem "A Glass-Ribbed Nest," later re-titled "The Paper Nautilus." Moore alludes to the depth of her interest in letter to Louise Crane (21 February 1937) thanking her for the present of the shell:

> It is well I did not know when I received the mysterious box, that a nautilus shell was inside, or my hand might have shaken so as to injure it. A nautilus has always seemed to me something supernatural. The more I look at it the less I can credit it,—this large yet weightless thing, with a glaze like ivory on the entrance and even on the sides. How curious the sudden change of direction in the corrugations, and the transparent oyster white dullness of the "paper." (*Selected Letters* 381)

BACK COVER: Marianne Moore. Moth. Watercolor. Sketchbook 1253/8. [1936-1937], XIII:03:10. Marianne Moore Collection, Rosenbach Museum & Library, Philadelphia. This sketch of a moth is one of many moth pictures Moore drew in the 1930s. She made it in Norfolk, Virginia, on a trip she and her mother took in the summer of 1936 to visit Warner (see also her mimosa sketch, above). Moths appear in the 1941 version (l. 34) of "Smooth Gnarled Crape Myrtle," and the 1936 version of "Walking-Sticks and Paperweights and Watermarks" describes "an invisible/fabric of inconsistency//motheaten by self-subtractives" (ll.17–19). However, during the 1930s it was certainly the butterfly, as she portrayed it in "Half Deity," that was the more significant insect in Moore's zoology. She did not forget the moths she repeatedly sketched in the thirties, however; in 1951, having entered decisively into the late phase of her work, she published "Armor's Undermining Modesty," a poem set into motion by:

> a moth almost an owl,
> Its wings were furred so well,
> with backgammon-board wedges interlacing
> on the wing—
>
> like cloth of gold in a pattern
> of scales with hair-seal Persian
> sheen. (*Complete Poems* 151)

WORKS CITED

Bishop, Elizabeth. *The Collected Prose*. Ed. Robert Giroux. New York: Farrar, Straus, 1984.

———. *One Art*. Ed. Robert Giroux. New York: Farrar, Straus, 1994.

Bornstein, George. *Material Modernism: The Politics of the Page*. Cambridge: Cambridge UP, 2001.

Holley, Margaret. *The Poetry of Marianne Moore: A Study in Voice and Value*. Cambridge: Cambridge UP, 1987.

Hyde, Lewis. *The Gift: Creativity and the Artist in the Modern World*. New York: Vintage Books, 2007.

Kappel, Andrew. "Complete with Omissions: The Text of Marianne Moore's *Complete Poems*." *Representing Modern Texts: Editing as Interpretation*. Ed. George Bornstein. Ann Arbor, U of Michigan P, 1991: 125–156.

———. "Presenting Miss Moore, Modernist: T.S. Eliot's Edition of Marianne Moore's *Selected Poems*." *Journal of Modern Literature* 19.1 (1994): 129–50.

Mayor, Alfred Goldsborough. *Sea-Shore Life: The Invertebrates of the New York Coast*. New York: New York Zoological Society, 1905.

McKerrow, Ronald B. *Printer's and Publisher's Devices 1485–1640*. London: Bibliographical Society, 1949.

Molesworth, Charles. *Marianne Moore: A Literary Life*. New York: Atheneum, 1990.

Moore, Marianne. *A-Quiver with Significance: Marianne Moore 1932–1936*. Ed. Heather Cass White. Victoria: ELS Editions, 2008.

———. *Becoming Marianne Moore: The Early Poems, 1907–1924*. Ed. Robin G. Schulze. Berkeley: U of California P, 2002.

———. *The Complete Poems of Marianne Moore*. Ed. Patricia C. Willis. New York: Penguin, 1981.

———. *The Complete Prose of Marianne Moore*. Ed. Patricia C. Willis. New York: Penguin, 1987.

———. *The Pangolin and Other Verse*. London: Brendin Publishing Co., 1936.

———. *The Selected Letters of Marianne Moore*. Eds. Bonnie Costello, Celeste Goodrich, and Cristanne Miller. New York: Knopf, 1997.

———. *What Are Years*. New York: Macmillan, 1941.

Redding, Patrick. "'One must make a distinction, however': Marianne Moore and Democratic Taste." Forthcoming in *Twentieth Century Literature*.

Schulze, Robin. "How Not to Edit: The Case of Marianne Moore." *Textual Cultures* 2.1 (2007): 119–137.

Slatin, John. *The Savage's Romance: The Poetry of Marianne Moore*. University Park and London: Pennsylvania State UP, 1986.

Stapleton, Laurence. *Marianne Moore: The Poet's Advance*. Princeton: Princeton UP, 1978.

INDEX OF POEMS

36, 121	Bird-Witted
51, 141	Four Quartz Crystal Clocks
58, 145	Glass-Ribbed Nest, A [The Paper Nautilus]
31, 88	Half Deity
20, 158	He "Digesteth Harde Yron"
18, 153	Light is Speech
53, 113	Pangolin, The
16, 150	Rigorists
47, 119	See in the Midst of Fair Leaves
34, 98	Smooth Gnarled Crepe Myrtle!
48, 155	Spenser's Ireland
29, 77	The Student
39, 101	Virginia Britannia
24, 123	Walking-Sticks and Paperweights and Watermarks
15, 148	What Are Years?

www.ingramcontent.com/pod-product-compliance
Lightning Source LLC
Chambersburg PA
CBHW060300240426
43661CB00060B/2852